BIRDS
of PREY

BIRDS of PREY

PAUL D. FROST

BARNES & NOBLE

NEW YORK

This edition published by Barnes & Noble Publishing, Inc.,
by arrangement with Parragon Publishing

2006 Barnes & Noble Books

M 10 9 8 7 6 5 4 3 2 1

ISBN 0-7607-8062-5

Printed in China

Designed, produced, and packaged by Stonecastle Graphics Limited

Text by Paul D. Frost
Edited by Philip de Ste. Croix
Designed by Paul Turner and Sue Pressley

PIEBALD EAGLE

Page 1: The very distinctive white head of the Bald Eagle (*Haliaeetus leucocephalus*) is only fully developed at seven years old. Juvenile Bald Eagles have brown heads which turn to a mottled color as the bird matures, before finally whitening. It is possible that the name Bald Eagle derives from a contraction of 'piebald' meaning 'brown and white,' or possibly from the Old English word 'balde' meaning white.

IN FOR THE KILL

Pages 2 and 3: Snowy Owls (*Bubo scandiacus*) prey mainly on small rodents, in particular lemmings and voles. Hunting is often done from a suitably high perch, which affords the owls a good view over the usually bleak terrain of the Arctic tundra which is their natural habitat. Prey is usually caught from above following the owl's silent gliding approach from its perch.

CONTENTS

INTRODUCTION

T his book not only sets out to inform its readers about a wide variety of birds of prey – the aerial predators of the world – it is also beautifully illustrated with many pictures which portray these impressive birds in their natural habitats in the wild.

Firstly, it is necessary to explain exactly what a bird of prey is. One dictionary definition suggests 'any of numerous carnivorous birds that hunt and kill other animals.' However, there are many carnivorous birds, such as the kingfisher family, that are not birds of prey. The feature that distinguishes carnivorous birds that are considered 'birds of prey' from all the others is the method by which they catch and kill their prey. Birds of prey use the sharp talons of their feet as their primary method of killing their prey, whereas other carnivorous birds tend to use only their beaks for this task.

Another term often used for birds of prey is 'raptor.' This comes from the Latin word *rapere*, meaning to seize and carry off. Sometimes the term is restricted to the diurnal (daytime hunting) birds of prey, such as eagles and hawks; however, this book accepts the more general definition, as given by the *Oxford English Dictionary*, which also includes owls.

When describing birds of prey, many exceptions crop up which make generalizations difficult. One of the first exceptions that we encounter concerns the definition of raptors using their feet to kill their prey. The

HIGH FLYING BIRD

The Rüppell's Vulture (*Gyps rueppellii*) holds the world record for being the highest flying bird. Unfortunately for the bird in question, it achieved this recognition by colliding with a commercial aircraft. The plane survived and the pilot recorded the height of the event – 37,000 feet (11,300m). The dead vulture was identified from feathers which had stuck to the aircraft.

PREVIOUS PAGES

Page 6: Tawny Eagle (*Aquila rapax*).
Page 7: Osprey (*Pandion haliaetus*).

vultures are predominantly carrion eaters, not killing their prey at all but feeding on the leftovers of other animals (though there are exceptions!), but they are still classified as birds of prey. Also, it is interesting to note that the vultures of North and South America are not related to any of the other birds of prey, but they are nevertheless considered as birds of prey for convenience and historical reasons. The definition also states that birds of prey are carnivorous, despite the fact that there is actually a vegetarian bird of prey, the Palmnut Vulture. The hawks and falcons are often classified as diurnal birds of prey, but there are some exceptions to this definition too. Generally female birds of prey are larger and more aggressive than the males, although again there are some species where this is not the case.

One thing that all birds of prey do have in common is remarkable eyesight. It is estimated that their eyesight is up to ten times better than ours. They are able to see in far more detail than we can and their eyesight is also far more sensitive to movement. Most of the diurnal raptors are believed to be able to distinguish color and some species can see a wider range of colors than humans, some well into the ultra-violet region of the spectrum.

All birds of prey have very sensitive hearing, though this feature is much more pronounced in owls than it is in diurnal raptors. Owls, more so than most of the other birds of prey, rely on sound to locate their prey. Their bodies and senses are specially adapted to help them achieve this goal.

The breeding and nesting habits of the different types of raptor make fascinating study. Many birds of prey mate for life, but there is rarely any sentiment governing this attachment. When one partner dies, it is not unusual for the remaining partner to start searching for a replacement mate within hours. They also exhibit very little attachment to their young. At an early age, sometimes only a matter of weeks after hatching, the young are seen by their parents as competitors for food and so they need to become fully independent very quickly.

Hunting techniques vary enormously. We are used to thinking of birds of prey as excellent fliers, soaring high and stooping and tirelessly chasing their prey on the wing. While some prefer the soaring and quartering techniques involving sustained flight, many raptors are not actually prepared to put that much effort into getting their food. Some favor 'still hunting' – sitting still on a suitable perch, waiting for the

THE EYES HAVE IT

All raptors have remarkable eyesight. Owls, such as this young Spotted Eagle Owl (*Bubo africanus*), can see much better than we can in very low light conditions, aided by a reflective layer behind the retina in the eye which acts to reflect light back onto the retina.

PREENING OSPREY

The Osprey (*Pandion haliaetus*) has a
highly developed preen gland near the
base of its tail which contains a
waterproof oil. It is important that
Ospreys have highly waterproofed
feathers as they often submerge
themselves fully when catching fish,
and regular preening maintains this
water-resistant coating.

THE DEVIL RIDES OUT

Opposite below: Though often seen
walking gracefully, Secretarybirds
(*Sagittarius serpentarius*) will
frequently lower their heads when
hunting and put on a high-speed
chase for prey. In some areas of Africa
the Secretarybird is more commonly
known as 'The Devil's Horse.'

prey to come within easy reach. Others prefer 'perch hunting,' making
short flights between suitable perches looking for prey in flight.

There are over 300 different species of diurnal raptor and over 200
species of owl. As current taxonomical studies of raptors evolve, using
new techniques, especially DNA analysis, the numbers of recognized
species is regularly changing, as is their classification. Often the different
techniques of classification give conflicting results, so different
authorities will disagree on what constitutes a true species.

When asked to list the various types of birds of prey, most people
would answer eagles, hawks, falcons, vultures, and owls. As this book
does not set out to be a definitive guide to birds of prey and their
taxonomical classification, the birds are here presented in those
popularly recognized groups.

Only two species and one family of birds do not easily fit into these
groups. The Osprey, though not an eagle, very much resembles one, so it
is included in that section. The caracaras are truly members of the
falcon family, but they are so different from typical falcons that it does
not seem appropriate to include them in that section. Consequently, the
caracaras and the Secretarybird are treated separately in this
introductory section.

Secretarybird

The Secretarybird is a very distinctive bird only found in Africa, in the grass plains and savannah south of the Sahara. It is the only bird of prey with predominantly terrestrial habits, walking anywhere up to 20 miles (32km) in a day. Despite rarely flying, Secretarybirds are actually very accomplished fliers when they need to be, using thermals to gain height and then soaring for great distances.

The main diet of Secretarybirds is snakes, lizards, grasshoppers, mice, birds' eggs, and the occasional small mammal. Accurately aiming a rear talon at the skull, the Secretarybird usually kills its prey with a very powerful stamp. Their height of over 4ft (1.2m) also enables them to kill some prey by repeatedly picking the creature up and dropping it onto hard ground. Often found at the edges of bush and grass fires, they will prey on anything that is fleeing to escape the flames, frequently also feeding on the carrion that has failed to escape.

Secretarybirds will usually mate for life. Once paired, they normally remain very close together, rarely straying out of one another's sight, although they do sometimes hunt in different areas. Their nests are normally built on the tops of tall trees, with both birds sharing the nesting responsibilities. The nests can be anywhere from 3 to 8ft (1-2.4m) in diameter and are very shallow. Females usually lay a clutch of up to three eggs. When the young birds hatch, unlike the majority of raptors, they exhibit no sibling rivalry, so if two eggs hatch, then both young are likely to survive.

I JUST FLUTTER MY EYELASHES

In addition to a third, inner, translucent eyelid (called the nictitating membrane) which helps to protect its eyes, the Secretarybird's eyelids are adorned with these remarkably long black eyelashes.

Also known as the Striated Caracara, Forster's Caracara (*Phalcoboenus australis*) is now only found on the Falkland Islands and a very few islands at the southernmost tip of South America. On the Falklands, the bird is more commonly referred to as Johnny Rook.

ON THE ROCKS

Right: The Crested Caracara (*Caracara plancus*) is the most widespread of the caracaras, found all the way from the southernmost tip of South America up into the southern states of the USA.

SMALL POPULATION

Opposite: In the Falklands, only 500–650 pairs of Forster's Caracara remain, and the population in mainland South America is probably even smaller.

Caracas

Nine species of caracara are generally recognized. They are often called 'carrion hawks.' They are found from Florida down to the Falkland Islands and Tierra del Fuego in the southern latitudes. They inhabit the various different environments of South America. The Red-throated Caracara lives deep in the tropical forests. The White-throated Caracara has been seen feeding high in the Andes alongside Andean Condors. The Striated Caracara is to be seen on the rocky coast of the Falkland Islands and other islands in the vicinity. The mostly widely distributed of the family, the Crested Caracara, is found in open countryside and on cattle-ranchland.

Despite being totally different in many ways, including appearance, flying style, diet, and behavior, they are very close relations of falcons.

The caracaras are characterized by their long necks and their yellow to reddish bare cheeks. They are very gregarious and aggressive. They are also very intelligent.

They spend much of the time scavenging on the ground, feeding mainly on carrion. They will eat reptiles, amphibians, and small birds, and the smaller species will eat insects. Though often seen near farms, Crested Caracaras more often than not feed on insects, grubs, and carrion, though some have developed the habit of attacking young livestock. In the late 1800s the Guadalupe Caracara also exhibited this characteristic, and this bird has the distinction of being one of the few species to be deliberately exterminated by man by the early 20th century.

Caracaras tend to nest either high in trees or on rocky ledges, though the Crested Caracara has been known to build nests on the ground or in cactuses.

LIFE IN THE TREE TOPS

Opposite: Secretarybirds (*Sagittarius serpentarius*) build their nests in the tops of tall trees. The nests tend to be broad but very shallow and lined with grass, wool, and animal droppings. Two or three eggs are laid in the tree-top nest and these are incubated by the female for about 45 days.

19TH-CENTURY SCRIVENER

Left: A Secretarybird stands upright displaying to good effect its gray body, black thighs, two black central streamers to its tail, and 20 black crest feathers on its head. Some people suggest that this visual combination resembles a 19th-century clerk or secretary wearing a tailcoat and knickerbocker trousers with quill pens placed behind his ears.

TAKE A LETTER

Right: Although the Secretarybird's distinctive head quills may resemble quill pens tucked behind the ears, it is more likely that the bird's fanciful name actually comes from a corruption of the Arabic words 'Saqu Ettair,' meaning hunter bird. It differs from all other birds of prey in that it kills by stamping with its long, powerful legs, using the short rear talon to crush with extreme force the base of the skull of its prey.

ONE OF A KIND

Opposite: The Secretarybird is the most distinctive of all of the raptors. Other than its diet, it has so little in common with any of the other birds of prey that it is classified as the only member of its family group.

A PRICE ON ITS HEAD

Forster's Caracara (*Phalcoboenus australis*) is not a particularly gregarious bird. Individuals are most likely to be seen either on their own or as a pair. At abundant food sources though, it is not unusual to see larger groups feeding and some birds may gorge themselves to the point where they are unable to fly. Forster's Caracara was known to occasionally attack sick or dying sheep, or to feed on their carcasses, which led to it being classified as a pest to sheep farming in the early years of the 20th century. The payment of a bounty for each bird killed led to a severe drop in the population. Now they are protected with heavy fines being levied on anyone found killing them, even if they are causing injury to livestock.

GENERAL SCAVENGER

Below: The Crested Caracara (*Caracara plancus*) mainly scavenges for carrion or injured prey. Most of its food is found by foraging on foot, and it frequently lifts small branches and stones in search of small prey. When searching for food on the wing, random low-level circling and gliding are used rather than any methodical search pattern being adopted.

OF NESTS AND NEIGHBORS

Right: Forster's Caracara (*Phalcoboenus australis*) make a small nest out of small sticks and grass either on a rocky ledge or on grassy tussocks. The nest is lined with wool, fabric, and soft materials. In areas where Forster's Caracara are quite heavily populated, it is not unusual for breeding pairs to nest in very close proximity to one another.

GOOSE STEP

Forster's Caracara often scavenge the edible trash from around farms and other inhabited areas. They are also known to prey on sick and young seabirds, particularly penguins. When other food is in short supply, they will attack and kill larger healthy birds, such as geese, either singly or in small groups.

EAGLES AND OSPREY

These are the most majestic of all of the birds of prey, and eagles are often referred to as the 'King of Birds.' They are the largest in stature of the typical birds of prey family, exceeded in size only by some of the vultures. The eagle has been widely accepted as a symbol of nobility throughout history.

What actually is an eagle? It is not an easy question to answer precisely. The term eagle is used to refer to a very diverse group of large birds of prey. The renowned authority on raptors, Dr. Leslie Brown, once humorously remarked that 'an eagle is a large or very large diurnal raptor which is *not* a kite, buzzard, vulture, hawk or falcon.'

Very similar to the buzzard (buteo) family of raptor, eagles are generally larger, though sometimes not significantly so. Eagles tend to be much more powerfully built than buzzards, regardless of their size. Like buzzards, they have broad rounded wings and a wide rounded tail, but they have larger feet and a much heavier beak. In flight, they are much more ponderous than buzzards and rely more on surprise to catch their prey, rather than pursuit.

Most eagles build their nests in trees, though in regions with very few trees, or where they are only small, the nest sites are likely to be on high mountain crags. The nest site is usually found on an elevated vantage point allowing the eagle to sweep into and out of it with ease. It is not unusual for a pair of eagles to have several nests within their territory, which are used in rotation. Where different species live in the same locality, it has been observed that occasionally an eagle of a different species will use an unoccupied nest within its territory.

NEST WITH A VIEW

Bald Eagles (*Haliaeetus leucocephalus*) almost always build their nests in tall trees near to open water. However, in the very northern reaches of their territory on the small Alaskan islands where trees are in short supply, they will build nests on the ground.

With the exception of the snake eagles, which make relatively small nests, eagles' nests tend to be large, fabricated from sticks and lined with leaves and other suitable soft warm material. Most of the nest building tends to be done by the female. Very often the nests are used from year to year, and each year new material is added both to the structure and the lining of the nests. One of the largest nests on record was made by a pair of Bald Eagles. It measured 10ft (3m) across and was 23ft (7m) high and weighed nearly two tons.

The average clutch size for the majority of eagles is two, but some, especially the larger eagles, lay only a single egg in any year. Incubation is performed mainly by the female, though the males will often share the job. Incubation takes around six weeks on average. If more than one egg is laid and hatched, it is not unusual for the older chick to kill, and even eat, the younger chick. Even if this doesn't happen, the older chick tends to be more strident in its call for food and consequently it gets a greater amount, growing faster and more strongly than its younger sibling.

The period of time before the young are fully fledged is, to a large extent, related to the size of the birds. Little Eagles are fully fledged in around seven to eight weeks on average, while harpy eagles take anywhere up to six months. The young are fully independent of their parents anywhere from a month after fledging up to more than a year in the case of young Philippine Eagles.

There are currently 68 species of raptor that are classified as eagles. Some authorities attempt to classify them into four main groups – true (or booted) eagles, fish (or sea) eagles, snake eagles, and harpy eagles.

True Eagles

This group consists of 32 species, including the smallest of all the eagles, the aptly named Little Eagle, found in Australia, which weighs less than 2lb (900g). They are often referred to as booted eagles, because their legs are thickly feathered all the way down to their toes, unlike most other eagles and buzzards.

CAMP FOLLOWER

The Tawny Eagle (*Aquila rapax*) usually feeds on fresh carrion, often the kills of other raptors, including mammals up to the size of rabbits. It will also hunt for small rodents, lizards and snakes, as well as locusts and grasshoppers. Tawny Eagles are often seen in the vicinity of hunting camps and they may follow hunting and shooting parties in the quest for food. They will boldly swoop down and snatch dead or injured prey before the hunters can collect it. The Indian Tawny Eagle (*Aquila rapax vindhiana*) is pictured below.

LITTLE VOICE

Opposite: Bald Eagles become most vocal around the breeding season but, despite their impressive size, they have rather weak voices. Lowering their heads and opening their beaks wide, the call that emerges sounds more like the cries of gulls.

SALMON LEAP

Below: In winter in North America, Bald Eagles often congregate in large flocks along coasts and rivers to take advantage of the abundance of spawning salmon and other fish. Despite the quantity of prey that is available at this time, Bald Eagles will still try to steal food from one another and from Ospreys.

The largest eagle in this group is also the largest eagle in Africa – it is the Martial Eagle, weighing up to 15lb (7kg). The best known of the true eagles is the Golden Eagle. It is found throughout much of the northern hemisphere and is remarkable in its range which extends from the frozen Arctic regions of Alaska down to the hot mountainous lands of the northern Sahara.

True eagles will feed on a variety of prey, including medium-sized birds and mammals ranging in size from rabbits and hares upward. Larger birds are able to catch and kill prey the size of a young deer or antelope. If available, they will also feed on carrion.

Fish Eagles

This group of ten eagles are all predominantly fish-eating. Unlike Ospreys, which are prepared to submerge themselves to catch their prey, fish eagles normally catch a fish by snatching it from near the surface of the water.

The best known of all this group is the Bald Eagle, the largest of the American eagles. It is found throughout most of continental North America, from Alaska through Canada and down to the southern states of the USA. As the national bird of the United States, it is recognized throughout the world. It is the archetypal eagle with large powerful wings, feet, and beak and an impressive noble appearance.

The largest of this group is Steller's Fish Eagle, found in eastern Asia. Females may grow to 44in (1.1m) in length with a wingspan of up to 96in (2.4m), with males being a little smaller. Steller's Fish Eagle is only marginally smaller in size than the Harpy Eagle, but is comparable in terms of its weight and wingspan.

Most of the fish eagles have varying amounts of white on their undersides; this affords them a large degree of camouflage when they are flying low over the water.

Snake Eagles

This group of 22 eagles are characterized by having a diet that predominantly consists of snakes. They are found mainly in Africa, India, China, and Indonesia, but the Short-toed Snake Eagle is migratory and spends summer throughout much of southern and northeastern Europe and parts of Russia.

In addition to snakes, they will also feed on lizards, frogs and other reptiles, small mammals, and occasionally crabs and fish. Most of the food is caught by the technique of 'still hunting,' with the birds often sitting on a partially covered branch by a river clearing, and dropping straight down on snakes as they pass underneath.

Harpy Eagles

This group of eagles consists of four species, which are the largest of all the eagles. The Harpy Eagle and the Crested Eagle are found in parts of Central and South America. The Philippine Eagle and the New Guinea Eagle inhabit the areas that their names suggest.

The world's largest eagle is the Harpy Eagle, which can weigh up to 20lb (9kg). A very close second is the Philippine Eagle, previously known as the Monkey-eating Eagle.

All four are forest-dwelling. They have relatively short, but extremely powerful, wings. They are able to lift and carry off prey that weigh almost as much as they do. They prey on large birds, forest-living mammals (including monkeys), and reptiles. In inhabited regions, they will take domestic livestock – Philippine Eagles have been reported as preying on young pigs and dogs from native villages.

Osprey

The Osprey is not considered as an eagle because in taxonomic terms it occupies a niche all of its own, apparently diverging from the rest of the birds of prey around 24-30 million years ago. However, because it looks and behaves very much like some of the typical fish-eating eagles, it would be capricious not to include it here.

The Osprey is found throughout much of the world, with the exception of central USA, northern Africa, and parts of southern Europe. It tends to breed only in northerly areas.

Ospreys prey almost exclusively on live fish, both saltwater and freshwater. They will only rarely take dead or dying fish. Unlike some other birds of prey, they are very unlikely to try to steal food from other birds, but occasionally their own catches are stolen by other birds, including herons.

Sometimes they locate their prey by 'still-hunting' from a perch, but more often they will glide and soar over a body of water, starting high and coming lower with each swoop. Once they have identified their prey, it will be caught with a feet-first dive, sometimes from a hover but more often from a glide. It is not unusual for an Osprey to submerge itself completely beneath the water to catch its prey, unlike fish eagles that just skim the surface. Some young Osprey can get into difficulty once submerged, lacking the strength to rise out of the water. As the Osprey flies off, it will usually adjust the position of the fish in its talons so that it comes out of the water head first – this reduces the drag of the water on the fish. Fish eagles, on the other hand, tend to bring the fish out sideways, holding it in both feet.

In order to get a better grip on slippery fish, the outermost toe of each foot is reversible and the undersides of the toes and feet are very

MONKEY EATER

At approximately 40in (1m) in height, the Philippine Eagle (*Pithecophaga jefferyi*) is the tallest, though not the largest, of the world's eagles. They mainly prey on large mammals, such as flying lemurs and macaque monkeys, and, because of this, they were previously known as the Monkey-eating Eagle. These impressive raptors often hunt monkeys cooperatively – one bird will distract the troop from the front while another picks off prey at the rear of the group. The Philippine Eagle is now close to extinction due to loss of habitat as a result of intensive agriculture.

scaly being covered with small sharp spicules (spines), which enable them to carry off prey weighing as much as 4lb (1.8kg).

Ospreys start to breed at three years old. They build their nests in the tops of trees (usually coniferous, if available), on rocky pinnacles or on artificial platforms. The nests are reused in subsequent years, being added to and relined, and as a consequence they can become very large. The normal clutch size is two or three eggs and incubation takes around five to six weeks. The young are fully fledged at around seven to eight weeks after hatching and they are independent of their parents within two months.

In the first year, up to 60 percent of the young population may die but those that do survive can usually live for 15 to 20 years. Some have been known to live for over 30 years.

FROM THE GROUND UP

Ospreys (*Pandion haliaetus*) construct their large nests by starting with a base of branches and very large twigs. Once the structure is complete, it is lined with any softer material that can be found locally, such as seaweed, reeds, grass, or heather.

GRACE AND POWER

With slow, deep, powerful beats of their very long, broad wings, Golden Eagles (*Aquila chrysaetos*) are particularly graceful birds in flight. They are also extremely powerful and have been seen soaring effortlessly in wind speeds of up to 100mph (160kph). When stooping from great heights onto their prey, they may even reach speeds close to those achieved by the fastest recorded animal, the Peregrine Falcon.

Despite widespread persecution by man in the 19th and 20th centuries which led to them at times being considered endangered in many regions, the Golden Eagle is thought to be very numerous globally. Found thoughout most of the northern hemisphere above the tropics, some estimates put the world population at 250,000 individuals.

LONE STALKER

Left: Golden Eagles use a variety of hunting techniques to catch their prey including soaring and stooping, 'still hunting,' and slow, low-level quartering. They have sometimes even been seen stalking slower-moving prey on the ground, approaching cautiously before jumping and grabbing the creature in their talons.

ELECTRIFYING

Above: In some areas of the USA one of the biggest threats to Golden Eagles is electrocution. Their wingspan can exceed 80in (2m). When gliding from electricity pylons their wings are wide enough to span a pair of cables, resulting in them suffering a massive electric shock. Some electricity companies have made modifications to their installations reducing deaths caused in this way by up to 95 percent.

CAIN AND ABEL

The female Golden Eagle usually lays two eggs separated by an interval of two days. Incubation starts when the first egg is laid, which means that it will hatch two days before the second egg. If both eggs hatch successfully, there is intense sibling rivalry. The older, larger chick kills and eats its younger sibling in up to 80 percent of cases.

OUT OF SIGHT

Above: The Martial Eagle (*Polemaetus bellicosus*) is the largest eagle found in Africa, at around 31-38in (79-97cm) in length. It spends much of the day in the air, soaring at such heights that it is only visible through powerful binoculars. Prey may be caught after a long slanting stoop stretching over a distance of as much as 3 miles (5km).

PICK OF THE CROP

Opposite: Martial Eagles will prey on a variety of mammals, birds, reptiles, and, occasionally, carrion. Large prey is eaten on the ground, often over a number of days. All diurnal raptors have a pouch in their throats called a crop, and this is clearly seen bulging in this picture. Food is stored in the crop and only passed into the stomach when the bird returns to roost. Indigestible parts of the prey, such as fur and bones, are regurgitated as pellets.

PIRATE EAGLE

Opposite and below: The Tawny Eagle (*Aquila rapax*) is a typically large member of the eagle family at about 24-28in (61-71 cm) in length with a wingspan of 65-73in (165-185cm). It has a reputation for stealing food from other birds, including other birds of prey, and can be considered a pirate among raptors. Left: When stealing food from other birds of prey, the Indian Tawny Eagle (*Aquila rapax vindhiana*) attacks from above while making continuous barking calls. A relentless tail chase often ensues until the other raptor drops its prey.

MONARCH'S EMBLEM

In the late 19th and early 20th century a representation of the Imperial Eagle (*Aquila heliaca*) was the heraldic emblem of the Austro-Hungarian monarchy. The largest of the European eagles, they measure approximately 27-33in (69-84cm) in length, with a wingspan of up to 87in (221cm). The Imperial Eagle is now threatened with extinction in Europe, where it is found only in a small region of Spain and some parts of southeastern Europe. The main population is now located in western and central Asia. Juvenile Imperial Eagles (above) take up to eight years to achieve their full adult plumage (opposite).

THE REIGN IN SPAIN

Although adult Imperial Eagles remain resident in Spain throughout the year, juveniles migrate to northern Africa for the winter. Now seriously threatened, conservation efforts had increased numbers from 30 breeding pairs in the late 1970s to 150 pairs by the early 1990s. However, by the end of the century numbers were in decline again. The main causes of this worrying trend are the use of agro-chemicals, collision with power lines, and illegal poisoning.

COLONIAL SUCCESS

The Wedge-tailed Eagle (*Aquila audax*) is found throughout Australia, including its desert regions. They often nest in densely forested regions, but hunt in open countryside. Forest clearing and the introduction of rabbits and sheep from the 19th century onward following the colonization of Australia proved highly beneficial to this eagle. Despite having been one of the world's most persecuted eagles – considered as vermin and with a price on its head in the 1950s – the population is believed to be higher now than it was before colonization.

A PAIR OF BOOTS

Above: Once paired, Booted Eagles (*Hieraaetus pennatus*) stay close to one another for much of the time. Even outside the breeding season, they will often hunt together. If one of a pair is seen alone, it is likely that its partner will be close by and will appear before long.

HAWK EAGLE

Right: Once thought to be a European and Asian variety of African Hawk Eagle, Bonelli's Eagles (*Hieraaetus fasciatus*) are now considered as a distinct species. They will often hunt like true hawks, such as the Goshawk, hiding in trees and darting out to catch unwary birds in flight.

SMALL BUT PERFECTLY FORMED

The Little Eagle (*Hieraaetus morphnoides*) is the smallest of the eagle family, being around 15-22in (38-56cm) in length. These small raptors are regularly mobbed by magpies and crows. Little Eagles nest in the tallest trees they can find, often using a disused nest of another raptor. Young Little Eagles are fully independent at around four months after hatching.

THE TUMBLER

Left and above: Bateleur (*Terathopius ecaudatus*). Bateleur is French for a tumbler, an acrobatic circus act. Despite their very short tails, these eagles are capable of highly agile aerial maneuvers when chasing prey, although they never somersault as their name suggests. Their very long wings also allow them to soar gracefully all day long. Rising on the morning thermals, they may cover more than 200 miles (320km) before descending at dusk to roost.

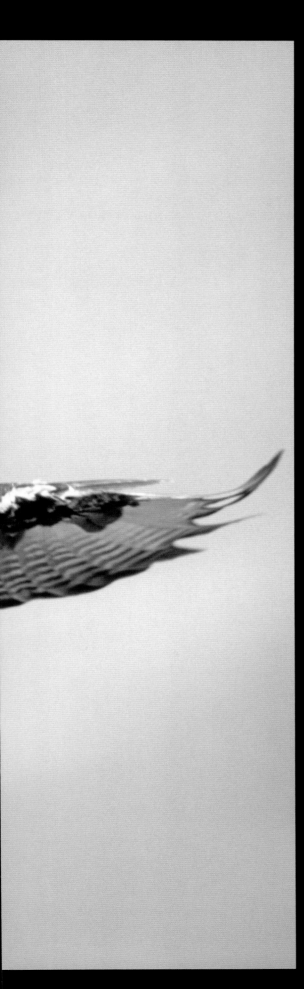

SPECIALIST HUNTER

Left and above: Verreaux's Eagle (*Aquila verreauxii*) is a highly specialized hunter preying mainly on the Rock Hyrax, a small, thickset, herbivorous mammal. In some areas of Africa, Rock Hyrax constitute up to 98 percent of the eagle's diet. The birds employ a variety of tactics to catch their prey. One method is to stoop down from soaring flight. Another is low-level foraging, often using the cover of rocks and ridges to launch a surprise attack from behind. They have even been seen to knock hyraxes from the tops of cliffs in order to kill them on the rocks below.

ALWAYS DIFFERENT

Above: As its name suggests, the Changeable Hawk Eagle (*Spizaetus cirrhatus*) is the most varied in appearance of all of the raptors. The six subspecies range in color from completely black to very light brown with darker flecks and spots. Their crest lengths vary too – one subspecies has no crest while another has a crest up to 6in (15cm) long.

WIDE-MOUTHED EAGLE

Right: Wintering in India and Africa, the same region as Tawny Eagles, Steppe Eagles (*Aquila nepalensis*) were once considered to be a possible subspecies. Now recognized as an entirely separate species, birdwatchers identify the Steppe Eagle by its wider mouth, which extends beyond the center of its eye – further than that of the Tawny Eagle.

AMERICAN ICON

In 1784 Benjamin Franklin reported his dismay at the Bald Eagle (*Haliaeetus leucocephalus*) being chosen as the national emblem of the USA. In his view it was a *'bird of bad moral character'* that did *'not get his living honestly.'* He observed that the Bald Eagle was too lazy to fish for itself, preferring to steal from other birds. He also noted that the Bald Eagle is a *'rank coward,'* often being driven out of its territory by the little King Bird, which is no bigger than a sparrow. He went on to extol the virtues of the Turkey as a *'much more respectable bird'* and a *'true original Native of America.'*

Most of the diurnal raptors, such as the Bald Eagle, have a pronounced bony ridge above their eyes, known as the 'supraorbital ridge.' This feature acts as a sun shade, reducing glare to give them a better view of any prey that may be present below.

GOING FISHING

The Bald Eagle mostly employs the technique of 'still hunting' from a high branch or cliff top. When a bird spots a large fish rising to the surface of nearby water, it makes a long shallow glide down to catch its prey.

HOOKED!

Unlike the fishing technique of Ospreys, Bald Eagles rarely plunge fully into the water to catch fish but almost always snatch their prey from just below the surface, barely wetting themselves in the process. In Alaska, dead or dying salmon are an important food source for Bald Eagles.

ENJOYING THE CATCH

Bald Eagles usually grab a fish with both feet using their sharp talons to grip it tightly, then lift it directly out of the water with no attempt to align the prey for a more streamlined exit from the water or for subsequent flight. The fish is quickly taken back to a tree or cliff-top perch to be eaten, with the bird taking care to look out for other Bald Eagles that might be tempted to try and steal its catch.

SUN IN ITS EYES

Above: Successfully reintroduced into Scotland over the last quarter of the 20th century, the bright yellow eyes of the White-tailed Fish Eagle (*Haliaeetus albicilla*) give rise to its Scottish name, *'Iolaire suil na greine,'* the 'eagle with the sunlit eye.'

BIG WHITE CHIEF

Right: The White-bellied Fish Eagle (*Haliaeetus leucogaster*) is found around the coasts of India, southeast Asia, and Australia. Their size and plumage make adult White-bellied Fish Eagles unmistakable. This juvenile will grow the full adult plumage of pure white head and body, with brownish gray wings and upper tail by its fourth or fifth year.

THE BIG FISHER

The largest of the fish eagles, Steller's Fish Eagle (*Haliaeetus pelagicus*) can weigh up to 20lb (9kg) which is approximately 50 percent heavier than the closely related Bald Eagle. They feed principally on fish, particularly salmon which have extremely tough skin which this eagle is well equipped to tackle with a specialized hatchet-like beak. When fish are scarce, they will also prey on birds and both land and sea mammals, including young seals.

DIFFERENT STROKES

Each of these snake-eating eagles has a different technique for catching its prey. Opposite: The Short-toed Snake Eagle (*Circaetus gallicus*), which is found in Africa and across Europe through to Russia and India, mainly forages with low-level quartering and circling but will often stoop from heights of between 500 and 1500ft (150-450m). Right: The Brown Snake Eagle (*Circaetus cinereus*) from sub-Saharan Africa prefers 'still hunting' from a tree or hillock and catches its prey following a long low flight. Above: The Crested Serpent Eagle (*Spilornis cheela*) from India, China, and southeast Asia also uses 'still hunting' from a tree branch, but sits motionless for long periods waiting to drop down onto prey passing below.

FLYAWAY CREST

Above: The well-named Long-crested Eagle (*Lophaetus occipitalis*) is unmistakable with its long, unruly crest of head feathers. Although occasionally taking farm poultry, they are generally welcomed in farmland areas of Africa where they prey mainly on mice and rats, which they catch using their small feet.

ELUSIVE GIANT

Right: The Harpy Eagle (*Harpia harpyja*) is the largest of the eagles, and may grow up to 35-40in (89-102cm) in length. Despite its size, it manages to stay hidden much of the time, dwarfed by the trees in the Amazon rain forest. The Harpy Eagle rarely soars above the treetops, but 'still hunts' or 'perch hunts' across clearings and rivers.

GAINING A TOE HOLD

Ospreys (*Pandion haliaetus*) will catch large fish of up to 4.5lb (2kg) in weight, often as a result of a stoop from a hover directly above the surfacing fish. Ospreys' feet are highly adapted to holding onto their prey. They have spiky scales on the underside of the talons, but, more importantly, all of the toes are the same length and the outer toe on each foot is reversible to ensure a very secure grip.

THE EASY WAY OUT

Left: As it rises out of the water, an Osprey maneuvers the fish it has caught so that it comes out of the water head-first. This reduces water drag making it easier to lift heavy fish. This streamlined position is maintained as the bird flies back to its perch to eat its prey. In 350BC the ancient Greek philosopher Aristotle observed that the Osprey 'grasps its prey with its talons, and often, from an inability to carry it, tumbles down into the water.' Over the last two thousand years Ospreys appear to have improved their fishing skills greatly, as they are nimble and efficient hunters.

FEED ME, FEED ME!

Above: Until they are able to fly and catch their own food, young Ospreys are fed mainly by the female parent with food caught by the male. Initially even the smallest fish will be pulled to pieces and fed in tiny portions to the young birds. As the young Ospreys grow larger, both the male and female will bring back fish that will be thrown whole into the nest for the young to feed themselves.

HAWKS

The term 'hawk' is used by most people to refer to those raptors that do not fit into the categories of eagle, falcon, vulture, or owl. The term covers a variety of both broad-winged birds of prey, such as the buzzards, kites, and harriers, and also the short-winged true hawks. These are very wide-ranging groups that vary significantly in hunting styles and types of prey.

Buzzards

There are 48 species of raptor that fall into this category, of which 28 are the true buzzards, often referred to as buteos. Typically buzzards are fairly large birds, though, on the whole, they are slightly smaller than eagles. Like eagles, they have very large, broad wings.

Most often seen in soaring flight in search of their prey, in order to gain height they will often search out thermals, rising on currents of warm air. By locking out their big broad wings, they can gain a lot of height, spiraling up in the thermals. The other main style of hunting employed by the buteos is 'still hunting.' Prey consists of small to medium-sized mammals, reptiles, amphibians, invertebrates, and large insects.

The largest of the family is the Ferruginous Hawk that is found throughout much of the western United States. Some weigh over 2½lb (1.1kg). The smallest is the Roadside Hawk weighing only 12oz (340g).

THE WAITING GAME

Although very capable aerial hunters, Red-tailed Hawks (*Buteo jamaicensis*) spend much of their time 'still hunting.' They perch high above the ground, intently inspecting the terrain around them as they wait for prey to come into sight and then swoop down to catch it. They feed mainly on small mammals, but are capable of taking hares weighing as much as 4.5lb (2kg).

PREVIOUS PAGES

Page 74: The Common Buzzard (*Buteo buteo*) is often mistaken for an eagle.
Page 75: The Roadside Hawk (*Rupornis magnirostris*) is found from Mexico down to northern Argentina, and it is the most common hawk found in those regions.

The most common of the buteos encountered in the USA is the Red-tailed Hawk. It is found throughout all areas of the United States, ranging from Central America, Cuba, Jamaica and the other large Caribbean islands all the way up through Canada to Alaska. Almost as large as the Ferruginous Hawk, it is a very aggressive, powerful hunter. Totally unconcerned by living in close proximity to man, these hawks are often found near farms, where they are often called 'Chicken Hawk.' They also live in more urban areas and have even been seen nesting in Central Park, New York.

Buteos usually build their own nests rather than inhabiting the disused nests of other birds. Nests are most often situated in trees but sometimes they are found on cliff edges. Very occasionally birds living in urban areas, such as the Red-tailed Hawk, will nest on man-made structures, such as skyscrapers. The nests are often used in subsequent years, being added to each year. The average clutch size is two or three eggs, but some birds will lay up to five when food is plentiful.

Very closely related to the buzzard family is the Harris' Hawk. In appearance it has the large broad wings that are typical of buzzards, but also the long legs that are characteristic of true hawks. In fact, its Latin family name, *Parabuteo*, means 'like a buzzard.'

Most raptors prefer either solitary hunting or, especially during the breeding season, hunting with their mate. However, the Harris' Hawk will very often hunt co-operatively in quite large, often family-based, groups.

Kites

There are 19 different species in the kite family. While it is known throughout most of the world, only two species are found in North America. The White-tailed Kite is resident in parts of South Carolina and California, while the Mississippi Kite is found in very localized areas of Kansas, Iowa, Tennessee, South Carolina, and Florida.

It is thought that kites are the oldest of the diurnal birds of prey from which all the others evolved. Part of the evidence for this theory comes from the fact that more predatory forms tend to evolve from less predatory forms – kites are the least predatory of the birds of prey. Kites feed mostly on carrion which is supplemented by snails, slugs, and earthworms. When kites prey on birds and mammals, it is often the very young or injured that are taken, rather than fit, healthy adults.

Soaring and low-level gliding, followed by very fast, agile swoops are the main techniques of predation used by kites. Large, broad wings coupled with relatively light body mass aid this style of searching and snatching carrion, which is often eaten on the wing.

The largest of the kites is the Red Kite, which breeds throughout much of Spain, France, Southern Italy, and in localized parts of the UK.

STREET CLEANER

In Britain during the Middle Ages the Red Kite (*Milvus milvus*) was a vital aid to public hygiene, feeding on garbage lying around towns and cities before it rotted, and so it was legally protected. As a result, the kite population grew to such numbers that they eventually needed to prey on domestic livestock for survival. In the 16th century the government declared that Red Kites were vermin and ordered that they should be killed throughout England and Wales.

FEARLESS THIEVES

The Black Kite (*Milvus migrans*) is a very bold scavenger with virtually no fear of humans. Black Kites often live in large numbers around towns and villages where they feed on discarded trash. In Africa and India they are regularly seen in market places swooping down and stealing food from cooking pots and even out of people's hands.

By the 19th century it was close to extinction in Britain, but a campaign started at the time and much revived in recent years involving the introduction of new stock from mainland Europe has seen the population grow back to viable levels. Unfortunately, there is still some persecution of these birds in some quarters. The kite is a carrion eater, but when the bird is seen eating a dead animal, it is wrongly assumed that the kite killed it. So instances of deliberate poisoning still go on, in spite of education campaigns to eliminate this practice.

The smallest of the kites is the Pearl Kite, which weighs less than 4oz (110g). It is found throughout tropical South America.

In terms of numbers, the most successful of all of the birds of prey is the Black Kite. With the exception of the UK, northern Scandinavia, northern Africa, and the Americas, it is found throughout the world. The Black Kite has no fear of man, often living in close proximity to humans and stealing food directly from people's plates. They will scavenge for food around garbage tips on the outskirts of settlements and even follow fishing boats, snatching fish that rise to the surface or are thrown overboard.

Kites usually build their own nests in trees and shrubs, and occasionally on rocky ledges or old buildings. Sometimes a nest will be constructed upon an old disused nest site. Clutch size on average is up to three eggs. Up to ten weeks can elapse before the young are fully fledged and they can remain dependent on their parents for a further ten weeks.

Very closely related to kites are the honey buzzards. Despite their name, honey buzzards feed mainly on the larvae of bees and wasps dug out of the nests or hives, rather than on honey itself. To shield themselves from stings, their faces are covered with a protective layer of small, very tightly packed feathers.

The most widespread of the five species is the Western Honey Buzzard, which is found in the UK and throughout Europe, southern Scandinavia, Russia, and parts of Asia. It is a highly migratory bird, overwintering in sub-Saharan Africa. In size and shape, it resembles the Common Buzzard. Early in the year before wasps and bees are active, birds will often feed on frogs and newts by snatching them out of shallow water. The usual hunting technique is 'still hunting,' waiting for foraging wasps. They will follow the wasps back to their nests; if the nest has been built in the open, the entire nest may be taken. Otherwise the buzzards will dig with their feet anywhere up to a depth of 16in (40cm) to expose the nest.

MAKING A BEELINE

Western Honey Buzzards (*Pernis apivorus*) breed late in the year so that the juvenile birds start to fledge just as wasps and bees are most abundant to provide them with a source of food. Shortly after fledging, they will migrate, sometimes covering distances in excess of 6000 miles (10,000km). The juvenile birds have much paler bodies than the adults, often with a white head and darker wings. They lose their juvenile plumage at their first molt.

REED BED

Below: Northern Marsh Harriers (*Circus aeruginosus*) usually build their nests on swamps or in thick vegetation above the waterline. They normally build a new nest each year using reeds, bulrushes, sticks, grass, and other vegetation. It can be as large as 2.5ft (80cm) wide and 10 inches (25cm) deep.

Harriers

There are 13 species of harrier. These birds are predominantly hunters of marsh and wetland regions, though they are found in many drier open localities, such as the pampas prairies of South America.

Harriers characteristically have long, slender wings, a long tail, and long legs. Their preferred method of hunting is by quartering their hunting territory with long gliding flights, to which their wings are ideally suited. Their long legs remain hanging low during these gliding flights in readiness to grab any prey quickly by surprise.

All harriers have a pronounced facial ruff, which indicates a significant reliance on sound to locate prey in the reeds and long grass that grow in the areas in which they hunt. They are often considered the diurnal counterparts of the short-eared owl family that frequently live and hunt in the same regions at night.

Harriers mainly prey on small wetland wading birds, small mammals, amphibians, reptiles, and large insects. In some regions the birds concentrate on particular prey that is present in abundance. Wintering in Africa, both the Pallid Harrier and Montagu's Harrier may feed there principally on migratory locusts.

OMNIVORE

The African Gymnogene (*Polyboroides typus*), or African Harrier-Hawk, enjoys a very varied diet. As well as eggs, young birds, frogs and other reptiles, insects, small mammals, and the occasional bat, they will often feed on oil-palm nuts. To reach the nuts, the bird carefully walks along the palm fronds steadying itself with its wings, appearing almost to use them to hold on. When the African Gymnogene is threatened, is hunting, or is in courtship displays, its bare face can rapidly change color from pale yellow to deep red.

With the exception of the Spotted Harrier from Australia, which nests in trees, harriers nest on the ground, often building fairly flimsy structures that are hidden amongst reeds or other vegetation. The females take on most of the responsibility for incubating the eggs and protecting the young in the first weeks after hatching. Despite needing up to seven weeks from hatching before they are fully fledged, the young often start straying from the nest at around two weeks because the nests are on the ground.

Closely related to the harriers are the African and Madagascar Gymnogenes or harrier-hawks. Similar in size to harriers, they are somewhat lighter with broader wings. In flight they are much more buoyant, making them look rather butterfly-like when in the air.

They take a very large variety of prey, often hunting on the ground. Eggs and young birds nesting in hollows of trees are particular targets. They will climb up to the nesting hole and reach inside it, taking advantage of the fact that their legs are double-jointed so they can bend in both directions to assist in finding food.

True Hawks

This group of raptors consists of 61 species, of which 47 belong to the Accipiter family, often referred to as true hawks.

Most of the Accipiters are woodland or scrubland hunting birds. Their short, broad, strong wings are suited to dashing between trees with great acceleration. Their long tails help them to change direction quickly to follow their prey as they dart between the trees.

The majority of these hawks prey on small to medium-sized birds, usually caught in flight after a brief dashing flight from a 'still hunting' perch. Other prey includes large insects, reptiles, and small mammals.

The largest of the true hawks is the Northern Goshawk, which weighs up to 5lb (2.3kg). It is found through much of the northern hemisphere. In the North American continent it is most often seen in Alaska and Canada and the northern and western states of the USA. It rarely appears in the southeastern states. In addition to medium-sized game birds, gulls, and waders, it also preys on a number of other raptors including the Honey Buzzard in Europe and many species of owl. It will catch mammals such as rabbits and both ground and tree squirrels. A ferocious hunter, sturdily built with very powerful legs, it can often catch and kill prey larger and heavier than itself.

The smallest of the true hawks is the Little Sparrowhawk, which weighs a mere 4oz (113g). It is found in southern and western Africa. In addition to smaller birds and mammals, these raptors will also prey on bats.

Most hawks build their own nests, though some will modify the disused nests of other birds. The nests are generally situated high up in trees. The average clutch sizes for hawks are between three and six eggs. The female looks after most of the incubation of the eggs. After hatching, the male is initially responsible for supplying the food for both the young and the female. As the young grow in size and require more nourishment, then the female will also help in providing food. The female is able to catch bigger prey because it is much larger than the male.

NOBLE HAWK

The name Goshawk derives from the Anglo-Saxon name of 'Goose Hawk.' The Northern Goshawk (*Accipiter gentilis*) is the largest of the true hawks or Accipiters and is a powerful, aggressive hunting bird. In Medieval England only noble men were allowed to own a Goshawk, which explains why the bird's scientific name is derived from the Latin words for noble (*'gentiles'*) and hawk (*'accipiter'*).

SMALL APPETITES

Common Buzzards (*Buteo buteo*) feed on a large variety of prey including worms, beetles, small birds, and mammals up to the size of small rabbits. They are content to eat around only half their own body weight in food each week and can even survive for several days without food. Many raptors, even some much smaller than Common Buzzards, need to eat up to three times their own weight in food per week to remain healthy.

RAINDANCE

Although often seen gracefully spiraling to great heights on thermals with its large wings spread wide, the Common Buzzard is a fairly lazy, sluggish bird, even in summer, and is most likely to be seen 'still hunting' from a fence post or similar perch. In dry weather, groups of Common Buzzards may often be seen in fields hopping from foot to foot to create the sound of rain, which encourages worms to rise to the surface. This unusual behavior has given rise to another colloquial name – Dancing Hawk.

HAWK OR EAGLE?

Opposite: The Ferruginous Hawk (*Buteo regalis*) has small feet but a very large mouth. This means that it can only catch small prey that is often quickly swallowed whole. Ornithological debate continues about whether or not it belongs to the Buteo family. If reclassified, it may change from its current status as the largest buzzard (buteo) in the USA to being considered the smallest eagle.

CHICKEN HAWK

Above: Despite rarely taking domestic poultry, the Red-tailed Hawk (*Buteo jamaicensis*) is often called the Chicken Hawk. They often build their nests in the fork of a tree, but in the absence of trees they will nest in cacti, on cliff ledges, and even on buildings in urban areas. When the young hawks have hatched, the adults will often bring more food to the nest than can be eaten, but any excess is taken away before it rots.

ECOLOGICALLY TOLERANT

Seen here flying high over the Grand Canyon, the Red-tailed Hawk is found widely over the entire North American continent. Red-tailed Hawks are prepared to inhabit practically any region that has trees to perch on and in which nests can be built. They are found in a wider range of habitats than any other member of the buzzard (buteo) family, and will even nest on giant cacti in desert regions.

ARCTIC BREEDER

Left and above: The Rough-legged Buzzard (*Buteo lagopus*) lives and breeds during the summer in the northernmost reaches of Alaska, Canada, Russia, and Scandinavia. Mostly nesting on the ground in the Arctic tundra, they will also build nests in the tops of tall, isolated trees if there are any in their breeding territory. The start of migration to and from the Arctic is dependent on the first snowfalls and the onset of snowmelt in spring.

MOUTHS TO FEED

The size of the Rough-legged Buzzard's egg clutch varies with the amount of food available. In years with little food, only two eggs may be laid, while in years with abundant food, there may be as many as seven. Once hatched, the male supplies all the required nourishment and survival of the young is dependent on his abilities to provide sufficient food. Within ten days of hatching, the first downy feathers of the young are replaced by a thicker set as protection against the Arctic cold.

CHILEAN BLUE

Opposite: Also called the Black-chested Eagle or, sometimes, the Chilean Blue Eagle, the Black-chested Eagle-Buzzard (*Geranoaetus melanoleucus*) is very closely related to the buzzard (buteo) family. As with eagle owls, the eagle part of the name refers to its large size rather than any genetic relationship with the eagle family of raptors. The Black-chested Eagle-Buzzard is much larger and bulkier than any of its close buteo relatives.

LONG-HAUL FLIGHT

Above: Swainson's Hawks (*Buteo swainsoni*) prey mainly on large insects and invertebrates, most often caught and eaten on the wing. Their long migration from North America to the La Pampa region of Argentina may take up to two months. Using soaring flight with very few wing beats, they can make the entire migration without feeding and only lose around a third of their weight in the process.

GO EAST, YOUNG HAWK!

Above: The Red-shouldered Hawk (*Buteo lineatus*) is common throughout many of the eastern states of the USA. On the western side of the USA they were previously only found locally in coastal regions from Oregon down to Mexico, but since the early 1990s they have been extending their range eastward and are now breeding in central Arizona.

THE WIND BENEATH ITS WINGS

Right: With a wingspan nearly three times its entire length and a very short tail, the Jackal Buzzard (*Buteo rufofuscus*) tends to rock from side to side as it flies, much like the Bateleur. The big, broad wings enable it to hang easily in updrafts of air prior to dropping down and catching its prey. Sometimes still referred to as the Augur Buzzard, these two species are now considered distinct.

KITING

Red-backed Hawks (*Buteo polyosoma*) hunt mainly from the air. By kiting into the wind they are able to maintain their position with very few wing beats, as they scan the ground for small mammals, mainly cavies. If no prey is spotted, they will glide on for a short distance and then resume their wind hovering. When a target is spotted, they stoop directly down upon their prey.

PERCH AND POUNCE

Above: Red-shouldered Hawks (*Buteo lineatus*) generally live in damp, deciduous woodland, often close to water and swamps. They generally use a 'perch and pounce' style of hunting – searching for prey while perched on a treetop, then dropping on to it from the air. They feed on a wide variety of reptiles, amphibians, and small mammals and occasionally fish, crayfish, and small birds.

NO WAY IN

Right: Even the very powerful feet of the Galapagos Hawk (*Buteo galapagoensis*) are incapable of breaking through the shells of adult tortoises. They are indigenous to the Galapagos Islands off the west coast of Ecuador and feed mainly on giant centipedes and locusts, although they will occasionally take hatchling tortoises and young iguanas.

BAY WINGED HAWK

Right: The Bay Winged Hawk (*Parabuteo unicinctus*) is found through much of South America (with the exception of the extreme south and the Amazonian forest), Central America, and parts of the southernmost states of the USA. The slightly larger but shorter-tailed subspecies found in the USA and Mexico, shown in this picture, is called the Harris' Hawk (*Parabuteo unicinctus harrisi*).

WOLVES OF THE SKY

Below: Sometimes referred to as the 'Wolf Of The Sky,' the Harris' Hawk is the only bird of prey that will hunt co-operatively as a group. Often a family group of parents and young will hunt together using a variety of sophisticated techniques to surprise or exhaust their prey.

MÉNAGE-À-TROIS

Opposite: Female Harris' Hawks will often take two male partners. Both males may mate with the female, although occasionally just one will, and both will be involved in rearing the young. A female with two males can successfully rear more young than two females with individual mates.

SUMMER HOLIDAY

Red Kites (*Milvus milvus*) are found through much of mainland Europe from the southern tip of Sweden down to the south of Spain and Italy. The more northerly birds migrate south over winter, while young birds usually remain in the warmer regions for their first summer, migrating back to their wintering regions in their second year.

BACK FROM THE BRINK

All pictures: By the late 18th century all Red Kites in England had been eradicated and only a small number remained in Wales. Unofficially protected by a concerned group of landowners from the late 19th century onward and now legally protected, the population in England and Wales is currently rising with the introduction of birds from Spain and Sweden. The female does most of the incubation and early rearing of the young, though she will sometimes go off and hunt for herself. While the female is absent, the male returns to the nest to incubate the eggs or to feed the young.

BESIDE THE SEASIDE

Black Kites (*Milvus migrans*) are often seen following fishing boats close to the seashore and in river mouths. Although they feed mainly on discarded fish and other scraps thrown overboard, on occasion they will snatch live fish from close to the surface of the water. Inland, Black Kites also gather in flocks around bush fires, and eagerly pounce on small animals as they attempt to escape the flames.

AFRICAN BLACK KITE?

Above: Currently the Yellow-billed Kite (*Milvus migrans parasitus*), which is found throughout sub-Saharan Africa, is considered a subspecies of the Black Kite. In addition to the yellow color of its beak (other Black Kites have black beaks), it is smaller and its body much less streaked in color than the Black Kites found through Europe, Asia, and Australia. It is under consideration for reclassification as a species in its own right.

NIGHT FISHER

Right: The Brahminy Kite (*Haliastur indus*) is sometimes found inland by rivers, lakes, and swamps but is more typically seen in the coastal regions of India, southeast Asia, and Australia. The white head and underside of the body are typical of fish-eating raptors. Mainly scavenging on waste, they will also sometimes catch fish from the surface of the sea or rivers. In Australia they have even been observed catching fish at night aided by the glow of harbor lights.

CUCKOO-FALCON

Above: Despite sometimes being called the Pacific Cuckoo-Falcon, the Pacific Baza (*Aviceda subcristata*) is a member of the kite family. Found mainly in forests and woodlands, it generally 'still hunts' for large insects from the cover of foliage.

WHISTLING IN THE DARK

Right: The Whistling Kite (*Haliastur sphenurus*) is aptly named after the distinctive whistling call that it makes throughout the day when perched and in flight. Indeed, it often continues whistling through the night. In common with other kites, it feeds mainly on carrion but in western Australia it is more predatory and is considered the main rabbit-eating raptor.

WALKING BOOTS

Western Honey Buzzards (*Pernis apivorus*) often forage on the ground looking for small mammals, beetles, and, sometimes, even berries. They have been known to walk for up to half a mile (800m) when foraging in this manner. Honey Buzzards may be distinguished from Common Buzzards by the dark, double bar marking near the base of their tails. Their wings are also longer and narrower than those of the Common Buzzard, and they have longer necks which accentuate their pigeon-like heads.

UP THE RIVER

Left: The main population of Northern Marsh Harriers (*Circus aeruginosus*) is found in Europe and Russia stretching across to northern Japan. Those birds living in colder regions migrate to Africa, India, and southeast Asia for the winter. When migrating to their winter habitats, they try to avoid flying over dry regions and follow coastlines and the course of river valleys as far as possible.

BEFORE NIGHT COMES

Above: Northern Marsh Harriers often amicably share the same territory as Short-eared Owls, hunting throughout the day while the owl hunts from dusk until dawn. Quartering its territory at a height of only a few meters above the ground, the Harrier's pronounced facial ruff helps it to locate small mammals and frogs in the vegetation by sound. Their large size makes them look deceptively slow, but they are able to fly at over 35mph (55kph) when hunting.

A WOMAN'S WORK

The female Northern Marsh Harrier is responsible for building the nest, incubating the eggs, and feeding the young. When the male brings food to the nest, he calls to the female who will leave the nest and, in a feat of mid-air acrobatics, catch the prey that he drops to her. Normally up to five eggs are laid, and when they hatch there is very little sibling rivalry between the smaller and larger birds, although if any die the surviving chicks will eat the carcass.

A BIT OF A BORE

Above: Until recently the Australasian Harrier (*Circus approximans*), previously called the Swamp Harrier, was considered to be a subspecies of the Northern Marsh Harrier. It is found throughout Australia, the whole of New Zealand, and on some Pacific Islands. They generally inhabit swamps, reedy lakes, and wetlands, but they are being increasingly seen in the desert regions of Australia where boreholes are now frequently sunk to tap underground sources of water.

TREE NESTING

Right: The Spotted Harrier (*Circus assimilis*) is the only species of harrier that makes its nest in a tree. Found mainly in Australia, they normally nest from July to December, but in the driest regions they may nest at any time during the year, depending both on rainfall and the availability of food.

HIGH MORTALITY RATE

Left: Hen Harriers (*Circus cyaneus*) usually lay between four and six eggs, at two-day intervals, so it can take up to two weeks to complete larger clutches. Incubation normally takes up to 40 days for an entire clutch to hatch, but the female will sometimes incubate infertile eggs for up to nine weeks. Often over half the eggs will fail to hatch and there is a high mortality rate among those that do hatch. Even with large clutches, it is not unusual for only one or two young to fully fledge.

SPEED CHANGE

Above: Hen Harriers generally prey on small or young birds and on small rodents and mammals. They usually hunt by quartering the same area every day, and they fly higher and faster when looking for birds to catch and lower and slower when hunting for rodents or mammals.

SOMETHING IN THE AIR

Left: The Pallid Harrier (*Circus macrourus*) preys mainly on small mammals, insects, and small birds, but the larger females will sometimes take bigger birds, such as ducks and grouse. Unlike the rest of the harriers which attack their prey on the ground, Pallid Harriers will often force birds into the air and then catch them on the wing.

FLOAT LIKE A BUTTERFLY

Above: The African Gymnogene (*Polyboroides typus*) is light for its size, weighing around 1.6lb (0.75kg), and it has very long, broad wings. In slow, low-level flight using frequent slow wing beats, it is easily buffeted about by the wind giving it a very butterfly-like flight. However, when soaring high on calm days with its wings spread out wide, it has a very steady and graceful appearance.

DOUBLE JOINTED

Although both the African and Madagascar Gymnogenes have double-jointed legs, enabling them to search inside cavities in trees for the eggs and young of nesting birds, the Madagascar Gymnogene (*Polyboroides radiatus*) spends more time foraging on the ground and turning over stones looking for beetles and insect larvae to eat than its mainland relative.

FAIR GAME

Northern Goshawks (*Accipiter gentilis*) sometimes prey on larger game birds, such as pheasants and grouse, but they are more likely to catch smaller birds, such as thrushes, starlings and pigeons. A single Woodpigeon provides sufficient food for a Goshawk for a day. Unfortunately, they are still persecuted in some areas because of the threat they are thought to pose to game birds.

IT'S BEHIND YOU!

Below: In addition to catching birds, the Northern Goshawk will prey on small mammals up to the size of tree squirrels. They mainly 'still hunt' from the cover of trees at the edges of woodlands, darting out and chasing their prey over distances of up to a third of a mile (500m).

PLUCKING POST

Opposite: Northern Sparrowhawks (*Accipiter nisus*) prey mainly on small birds which are caught in surprise attacks on the wing. Scattered feathers and other remains of prey in wooded areas often indicate the presence of a Sparrowhawk. When they have caught their prey, they will often take it to a nearby perch and pluck the bird before feeding on it.

BIRD TABLE FASTFOOD

Above: In urban areas where many people have bird tables in their gardens, Northern Sparrowhawks will often treat them like drive-in restaurants. Hiding in hedgerows at the edges of gardens, they will intently watch and make fast dashes to grab small birds feeding on the tables. They are often so intent on their prey that they may accidentally collide with windows and glass doors.

RECYCLING

Right: Northern Sparrowhawks usually build a new nest each year. Quite often they will dismantle an old nest and reuse the building material. They build their nests in trees, at heights from 10ft to 100ft (3-30m) above the ground. During incubation and early rearing of the young, the male usually hunts for food at some distance from the nest, so it is not unusual for other prey species to nest safely in close proximity to them.

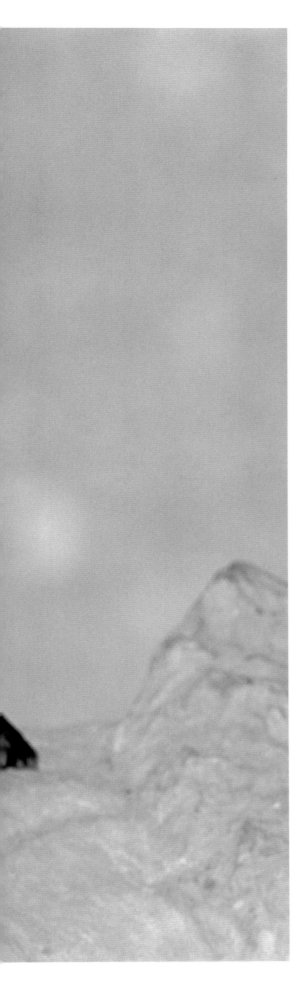

NO FEAR

Left: The Gabar Goshawk (*Micronisus gabar*) is a close relative of the true hawks (Accipiters) and is more often mistaken for a sparrowhawk than recognized as a goshawk. Found mainly in the savannah and acacia bushveld regions of sub-Saharan Africa, it is now also colonizing more built-up areas. These small, bold birds have little fear of man, and so will often be seen close to people, preying on other small birds that are disturbed by human activity.

TO THE BAT CAVE

Above: The Crested Goshawk (*Accipiter trivirgatus*) is among the largest of the true hawks and measures around 12-18in (30-46cm) in length. They live in the forest regions of southeast Asia and prey mainly on birds, lizards, and mammals. They will often specialize in catching prey that is abundant in their particular territory – those living around caves in Borneo, for instance, prey mainly on bats that fly at dusk and dawn.

NOISY NEIGHBORS

Opposite: The Shikra (*Accipiter badius*) is the noisiest of all the true hawks, having a range of several different calls that are made continually. During the breeding season they become even noisier. They feed mainly on lizards and insects, and it appears that their constant calling does not significantly disturb their prey.

YOU HAVEN'T SEEN ME

Above: The Brown Goshawk (*Accipiter fasciatus*), also known as the Australian Goshawk, hunts using secretive, silent, skulking movements. It often approaches its prey using a series of short flights through thick vegetation before pouncing directly down onto the victim. In southern parts of Australia these birds prey mainly on rabbits, but in other regions they will feed on reptiles, amphibians, and birds up to the size of young herons.

140

ON SONG

Above: The Pale Chanting Goshawk (*Melierax poliopterus*) is found through much of south and southwest Africa, while left: the Dark Chanting Goshawk (*Melierax metabates*) is found throughout much of the remainder of sub-Saharan Africa. Throughout most of the year they are very quiet birds, but when the breeding season starts, the males of both species will find a high, conspicuous perch on which to sit and from where they will make a melodious chanting call often lasting for several hours at a time.

POLE PERCHER

Opposite: Unlike many of the other true hawks, as well as hunting from cover, Cooper's Hawks (*Accipiter cooperii*) will often 'still hunt' from more exposed vantage points, such as telephone poles. In some areas they have even been seen stalking and flushing game birds on foot.

SMALLEST HAWK

Above: The Sharp-shinned Hawk (*Accipiter striatus*) is the smallest true hawk in the USA, measuring about 9-14in (23-36cm) in length. They breed as far north as central Alaska and each year they migrate south following the same routes. At Hawk Mountain, Pennsylvania they exhibit the most prolonged migration period of any species, starting in mid-August and continuing until late October and often even later than that.

WORLDS APART BUT MUCH THE SAME

Left: Lizard Buzzard (*Kaupifalco monogrammicus*) and above: White Hawk (*Leucopternis albicollis*). Occupying similar niches on different continents, these two hawks are old and new world counterparts of one another. The Lizard Buzzard comes from sub-Saharan Africa and the White Hawk is found from Central America down to the middle of South America. Both species live in woodlands and exhibit a preference for clearings rather than dense forest. They both prey predominantly on reptiles such as snakes, which are mainly caught by 'still hunting' techniques.

FALCONS

The falcons are the kings of speed of the raptor world. The Peregrine Falcon is on record as achieving the fastest speed of any animal. Excluding caracaras, there are currently 54 known different species of falcon, consisting of 39 species of true falcons plus pygmy falcons, falconets, forest-falcons, and the Laughing Falcon.

The smallest of the falcon family is the sparrow-sized Black-thighed Falconet found in Indonesia and Malaya, which weighs between 1 and 2oz (28-56g). The largest is the Gyr Falcon. This is found during summer above the Arctic Circle, while it winters as far down as the US/Canadian border and northern Scandinavia. Female Gyr Falcons may weigh anywhere up to 4.5lb (2kg).

The word falcon derives from the Latin word 'falco' meaning scimitar-shaped – a reference to the shape of their wings. Falcons have long narrow wings, which are swept back from the body enabling them to fly very fast.

In addition to the characteristic wings, most falcons have a notch in the upper beak. Called the 'tomial tooth,' there are suggestions that this may be a vestigial tooth left over from their reptilian ancestry. If their prey is not killed outright by their attack, falcons will administer a final *coup de grâce* by biting the victim's neck. The notch is ideally suited to fitting around and breaking the neck of small prey.

TEMPERATURE TOLERANT

The African Peregrine Falcon (*Falco peregrinus minor*) is the most widespread of the larger falcons. They are able to withstand temperatures that range from the intense cold of the Arctic to the blistering heat of the tropical regions of South America and Africa.

PREVIOUS PAGES

Page 146: The strikingly-marked American Kestrel (*Falco sparverius*). Page 147: By use of a hi-tech, low-weight speedometer attached to its tail, a Peregrine Falcon (*Falco peregrinus*) has been clocked at a top speed of 242mph (389kph) in a stoop, making it the fastest recorded animal.

Most falcons also have a dark strip of feathers below the eyes extending downward from the beak, looking somewhat like a mustache. Known as the 'malar strip,' these dark feathers reduce the effect of glare in the birds' eyes.

Unlike many other birds of prey, falcons rarely eat carrion, preferring freshly caught prey. They rely both on speed and agility to catch their prey, generally hunting smaller birds that are caught in flight. Many falcons have an elongated middle toe, which is often used to help grasp prey while in flight.

Falcons rely on several strategies to catch their prey. Kestrels, in particular, use hovering and stooping as their preferred hunting method. Another technique is to use low-level chasing, rising at the last moment to catch the prey from above. The method of predation that most people associate with falcons is the strike from above – they gain great height and then stoop from altitude and hit the prey at high speed.

When stooping in this way, falcons use thermals to gain height and then soar in search of their prey. Once it is located, they drop down toward it, often using powered flight (flapping their wings) to increase their speed, and at the last moment they level off to strike the prey at high speed, usually from behind. Some falcons will approach their prey

HOVER CRAFT

Left: The Common Kestrel (*Falco tinnunculus*) is the only bird of prey that can perform a sustained true hover – remaining motionless above the ground using flapping motions of its wings to maintain its position, even in still air. Along with other raptors, its preferred method is 'wind hovering' – facing into the wind with wings and tail set at the correct angle to remain stationary aloft with minimal flapping.

THE TRAIL'S TALE

Below: When leaving their nests for food, voles mark their trail with urine, which is highly reflective of ultraviolet light. Common Kestrels are able to see well into the ultraviolet spectrum and, hovering above, the vole's bright tell-tale trail enables the Kestrel to locate its prey with ease.

with their toes bunched tight like fists, and held close to the body, punching out at the target as they pass. Other falcons will approach the prey with their feet facing forward, striking it with the base of the foot. This has the effect of bending the foot around so that the rear talon rakes through the prey, sometimes taking the head clean off smaller prey. Whichever technique is used, within a fraction of a second of the strike falcons are able to grasp the prey with their elongated toes. On the occasions when they miss an outright kill, they will chase the prey down, often catching it before it hits the ground. If not already dead, it will be despatched with a quick nip to the neck.

The smallest members of the falcon family, pygmy falcons and falconets, are found in parts of Africa, India, China, and the Indo-Malayan regions. They have the notched beak and elongated toes that are characteristic of the main falcon family, but they are only capable of catching much smaller prey. While these little raptors will feed on small birds, their diet also consists of insects, including butterflies, moths, and dragonflies. Occasionally they catch small reptiles and mammals. Rather than using the high-flying and stooping techniques of hunting, they usually perch above the ground waiting for their prey and then quickly dart out when it is spotted.

SPEED KILLS

Mainly catching birds in flight, Peregrine Falcons (*Falco peregrinus*) are capable of killing prey over twice their own weight. The sheer speed at which they strike their prey will often kill it outright. Here, a Peregrine Falcon is seen on a dead pheasant.

South America is home to some far less typical members of the falcon family, the forest-falcons and the Laughing Falcon. Living and hunting in forested areas, their wings tend to be shorter than those of the true falcons. Their toes also tend to be shorter and they all lack the characteristic notched beak. These latter variations reflect differences in their prey. Like some owls and harriers, forest-falcons have a slight facial ruff, which may indicate that they rely on sound to locate their prey to a greater degree than true falcons do.

Forest-falcons feed on a variety of prey, much like the buzzard (buteo) family. The diet includes most small prey animals that abound in tropical forests, including lizards, insects and beetles, frogs, small birds, and crabs. Forest-falcons use a variety of hunting techniques including 'still hunting,' 'perch hunting,' and foraging on the ground looking for prey. Two species, the Slaty-backed Forest-Falcon and the Collared Forest-Falcon, are thought to have a special call which is difficult to locate but which induces a mobbing response in small birds. This reaction allows them to locate their prey easily.

The Laughing Falcon preys predominantly on snakes of both harmless and venomous varieties. It mainly uses 'still hunting' to catch its prey. As the snake passes, it will pounce down and catch the snake behind the head with its feet and then render the snake harmless by biting off its head. The snake will be eaten on a feeding perch, rather

IT'S ALL IN THE TIMING

Most falcons catch their prey from behind, but the Lanner Falcon (*Falco biamarcus*) will regularly attack its prey head on. As the relative approach speed between falcon and prey is greatly increased by this tactic, exceptional agility and timing are required by the Lanner to ensure a clean strike and kill.

ON THE LEDGE

The Peregrine Falcon's (*Falco peregrinus*) favored nesting site is on the steep sides of cliffs. Sometimes they use a simple 'scrape' on bare rock as a nest, although they will often occupy the disused nest of a different bird. In urban areas, Peregrines select balconies on skyscrapers, ledges on churches and cathedrals, and crevices in tall chimneys as suitable nesting sites.

than on the ground; smaller snakes will be carried in the beak, larger snakes in the feet.

Falcons almost never build nests of their own. Many take over the disused nests of other birds. Some lay their eggs in small scrapes on cliff ledges; others use hollows in trees. Some falcons that live close to man-made structures will use those too. There have been many reports in recent years of Peregrine Falcons nesting on the tops of tall buildings, such as skyscrapers, in very close proximity to people. In Britain and Europe, the Common Kestrel regularly hunts along the verges and central reservations of freeways. They have even been found nesting in structures located along the freeways, including roadsigns. Due to the bird's protected status in the UK, a pair of Common Kestrels even brought major road repair work to a halt for several months by nesting underneath a freeway bridge.

The average clutch size of a falcon ranges from three to five eggs, though some will only lay a single egg while clutches of up to nine have been recorded for some species. The eggs are normally laid at two- to three-day intervals. The female mainly looks after incubation, and for most species this lasts in the region of four to five weeks. The young are fully fledged anywhere from four to eight weeks after hatching.

While some young birds are dependent on their parents for a few weeks after fledging, others, such as the Lesser Kestrel, may only be dependent for about one week. One instance has been recorded of full independence in only two days! At the other end of the spectrum, the young of the Seychelles Kestrel may remain dependent on their parents for nearly six months after fledging.

Once they achieve independence, most young will stay in the region of the nest site for up to a month. However some, like young Barbary Falcons which are fully independent eight weeks after hatching, may stay with their parents for a further three months. During this period it is not unusual for groups of juvenile birds to form social hunting groups. Where stooping is a favored method of hunting, the young will often accompany the parent birds which catch small prey and then fly above the young and drop the prey in order to encourage the stooping behavior in their offspring.

FAST LEARNERS, BIG EATERS

In the first few weeks of life, young Peregrine Falcons are completely dependent on their parents for food. Usually the male will provide prey, which will be fed to the young by the female. As the young birds grow, both parents may need to hunt to provide sufficient food for them. Fledging can take place at around five to six weeks, when the parents will start to teach the young to hunt for themselves.

ARCTIC HUNTER

Opposite: The largest of the falcon family is the Gyr Falcon (*Falco rusticolus*) which is about 20-25in (51-63cm) long with a wingspan of up to 52in (132cm). They spend the summers in the Arctic regions and rarely migrate below the US/Canadian border in winter. Much of their bulkiness is a result of the thick feathering, especially on the belly and thighs, which is required to conserve heat.

JUVENILE COLORS

Above: Adult Gyr Falcons are mostly light gray in color, although they may vary from almost pure white-fronted with dark markings on the chest through to completely blackish-brown with white streaks. The young birds are more highly marked in their first year and only achieve their full adult plumage after two moltings.

LOCAL PRODUCE

With only limited food sources to be found in the Arctic region, Gyr Falcons must rely on what is available locally. In some regions the diet consists mainly of birds from the size of small finches to large geese and Capercaillie. In other regions the food is predominantly mammals, including voles, hares, and lemmings. Ground-hugging chases over several miles may be required to catch some fast-moving prey.

LOW DOWN AND SNEAKY

Above and right: The Saker Falcon (*Falco cherrug*) preys mainly on small- to medium-sized mammals, such as hamsters, gerbils, and hares. Scanning for prey from a high vantage point, Sakers swoop down to make low-level surprise attacks on their victims, which may be carried up and eaten in the air if small enough.

DON'T HOLD YOUR BREATH

Opposite: The dark feathers below the eyes of Saker Falcons form the 'malar strip' which reduces the reflection of light into their eyes, so improving vision. In the bird's nostrils, a system of baffles help to equalize the changes in air pressure experienced in stoops so enabling the bird to breathe during fast maneuvers.

HAWKING FALCON

Above: In addition to high-speed chasing of birds in flight, a Lanner Falcon (*Falco biamarcus*) will also employ much slower, hawk-like flight techniques to catch slower-moving prey, such as large insects.

FAVORITE SEAT

Opposite: Many Lanner Falcons have favorite places from which to hunt, and they will often spend much of the day soaring near a favored perch, such as a particular rocky crag. When not flying, they will also spend a good deal of time sitting on that spot surveying the area for suitable prey.

FLY CATCHER

Above: The falconets are the smallest
of the falcon family at around 5.5-7in
(14-18cm) in length. Collared
Falconets (*Microhierax caerulescens*)
live in open woodland or at the edges
of forests where they mainly prey on
flying insects, especially butterflies,
moths, and dragonflies. They employ
a 'still hunting' technique – they perch
on branches, waiting to dart out, grab
their prey and return to the same
branch to feed.

CLEAR SKIES OR CLOUD COVER

Right: On hot, sunny days, Peregrine
Falcons (*Falco peregrinus*) will use
warm thermals in the air to gain
height in order to hunt while soaring
or circling at altitude. In cloudy or
cold conditions, they are equally
happy to employ the 'still hunting'
technique (sitting still on a perch and
waiting for prey to venture near them)
from a suitably high vantage point.

MANTLEPIECE

Opposite: Once caught, if the
Peregrine Falcon's prey is too large to
carry off, then it is in danger of being
stolen by other predators, including
other raptors. The natural behavior of
all raptors is to 'mantle' over the prey,
hiding it by spreading their wings and
hunching over it, as seen here.

THE WANDERER

Above: Cassin's Peregrine Falcon (*Falco peregrinus cassini*) is the most
southern subspecies of Peregrine Falcon, but also one of the most widely
traveled. Although they spend most of their time at the southernmost tip of
South America and in the Falkland Islands, some have journeyed as far north as
Colombia during winter.

BACK FROM THE BRINK OF EXTINCTION

Opposite: The Mauritius Kestrel (*Falco punctatus*) is a spectacular example of successful conservation at work. By the mid-1970s there were only four known Mauritius Kestrels living in the wild. A concerted breeding and reintroduction program raised the numbers in the wild to over 800 within 25 years and in 2000 it was no longer considered an endangered species.

COLOR CODED

Above: While many raptors show no color difference between males and females, the Australian Kestrel (*Falco cenchroides*) is similar to the Common Kestrel in displaying a noticeable variation between the sexes. Male Common and Australian Kestrels have gray heads and tails, while the females are brown all over. Young males resemble females until their second full molt.

A CHANGE OF STYLE

Above: American Kestrel (*Falco sparverius*) and right: Common Kestrel (*Falco tinnunculus*). Hovering in flight to hunt consumes a lot of energy, so kestrels will often prefer 'still hunting' from a high perch, followed by a drop and glide to catch their prey. Kestrels eat small mammals, as well as a variety of ground-based prey including insects, beetles, and earthworms. Once commonly known as the Sparrow Hawk because of its small stature (it is only 7.5-10.5in [19-27cm] in length), the American Kestrel is actually a true falcon. Unlike most falcons,

HOBBY HORSE

Left: The Northern Hobby (*Falco subbuteo*) is very fast and acrobatic in flight and is one of the very few birds of prey capable of outflying swifts, at speeds approaching 100mph (160kph). Its name is thought to derive from the Old Dutch word 'hobben,' meaning to toss or to move up and down. This is the same word that gives us the derivation 'hobby-horse.'

CROWS' NEST

Above: Highly migratory during winter and a regular visitor to Africa, the Northern Hobby returns to Europe and Russia during spring and summer. Here they breed and rear their young in disused nests, often those of Carrion and Hooded Crows.

BIG GIRLS, LITTLE BOYS

In almost all instances, female raptors are larger and more aggressive than their male counterparts, and the Merlin (*Falco columbarius*) is no exception. Known scientifically as reverse size dimorphism, the size difference is more pronounced in falcons than in any of the other raptors. Females (opposite) can be over a third larger in size and weigh half as much again as the males (above).

GO SOUTH, YOUNG BIRD

Opposite: Young Merlins usually take their first flight within four weeks of hatching, and their flying skills develop rapidly. Merlins breed throughout northern Europe, Asia, and North America. Around six weeks after fledging, they will set out on their long migration south for the winter.

BETWEEN THE TREES

Right: The wings of the Lined Forest-Falcon (*Micrastur gilvicollis*) are much more rounded than those of most other falcons, which are generally pointed. They are well adapted to hunting in forests, and the birds appear to prefer a woodland habitat, flying around the edges of trees, rather than across open ground. Very often they will hunt on foot, catching small mammals on the ground, rather than chasing small birds in flight.

DAWN AND DUSK FEEDERS

Right: Bat Falcon (*Falco rufigularis*) and below: Aplomado Falcon (*Falco femoralis*). Both Bat Falcons and Aplomado Falcons are dawn and dusk (crepuscular) hunters. Both species feed on a diet consisting mainly of small birds, large insects, and some bats. Most prey is taken on the wing in the open, following a tail-chase. Aplomado Falcons will hunt cooperatively with their mates more than any of the other falcons.

DEMENTED HEN

Opposite: The Brown Falcon (*Falco berigora*) is noted for its very loud and distinctive call. This resident of Australia, Tasmania, New Guinea, and Dampier Island sounds much more like a parrot than any other raptor, and has a call that has sometimes been likened to that of a 'demented hen.' Its diet consists of insects and small mammals up to the size of a rabbit, supplemented on occasions by young birds, lizards, and snakes.

HOODWINKED

Peregrine Falcon (*Falco peregrinus*). Most of the predators of falcons are nocturnal, and they rely mainly on sound to locate their prey while they roost at night. The falconer's habit of using a hood to control his falcons stems from the raptor's natural instinct to be still and quiet in the dark, so that it may remain safe from predators. They are hoodwinked by the falconer into thinking it is night time during the day.

VULTURES

These birds are Nature's sanitation workers. They are
predominantly carrion eaters, picking clean dead carcasses
before they begin to rot and potentially create a health hazard.
In addition to feeding on carrion, many are also scavengers and are
consequently often found near population centers, feeding on garbage
tips that are often situated at the edge of towns.

There are two groups of vultures: the new world vultures found in
North and South America and the old world vultures found in Africa,
Asia, and Europe. The provide an excellent example of what is known
as 'convergent evolution:' despite many similarities, such as diet and
their bald heads and necks, the two groups are unrelated. New world
vultures are more closely related to storks and herons than to any of the
members of the raptor family.

The vultures are the oldest of the diurnal raptors. Fossil records of
new world vultures date back to some 50 million years ago and those of
old world vultures to around 30 million years ago. Fossils of both old and
new world vultures have been found in Europe and the Americas. Why
the new world vultures became extinct in Europe and the old world
vultures became extinct in the Americas is, to this day, a mystery.

One of the major differences between the two groups can be seen in
their feet. New world vultures have much smaller feet, more suited to

NOT SO DIRTY BUZZARD

Along with other vultures, the Turkey Vulture (*Cathartes aura*), or Turkey Buzzard, has the reputation of being a dirty bird. Even though their diet is carrion, they prefer not to eat rotten flesh, however, concentrating mainly on the fresher parts. After feeding, they usually bathe and often spend up to three hours preening themselves.

PREVIOUS PAGES

Page 180: The brightly colored King Vulture (*Sarcorhamphus papa*).
Page 181: The Lappet-faced Vulture (*Aegypius tracheliotus*) is an old world vulture that lives in central and southern Africa.

walking than to killing. Despite rarely killing with them, old world vultures' feet are much more similar to those of other raptors.

New World Vultures

There are seven species of new world vulture: the Andean Condor, the Californian Condor, the King Vulture, the Black Vulture, the Turkey Vulture, and the Greater and Lesser Yellow-headed Vultures.

The Andean Condor may be ranked as the largest of all flying birds. While the Maribou Stork and the Wandering Albatross both have slightly larger wingspans, the Andean Condor is much heavier than either. The Californian Condor comes a very close second to the Andean Condor in terms of both wingspan and weight.

Condors only breed every other year. The female Andean Condor lays two eggs whereas the Californian Condor only lays a single egg. The eggs are usually laid on the ground amongst boulders or in hollows on mountain cliffs or remote ledges. These 'nests' are normally situated close to large trees where the adults can roost. The young stay in the 'nests' for around 20 weeks, but then spend the next seven months running around on the ground before they are able to fly and hunt for themselves. They are dependent on the parent birds for up to another seven months. Condors take around five to six years to mature into fully developed adults.

Other than the King Vulture, which lays its eggs in crevices in trees, other new world vultures also lay their eggs directly on the ground, usually on cliff ledges which are fairly inaccessible to other animals.

By the early 1980s, the population of Californian Condors had dwindled to 21 known birds, both wild and in captivity. Since then a captive breed and release program has significantly increased the wild population, but it is still far from being secure.

Unlike other birds of prey, Turkey Vultures (and to a much lesser extent, the Greater and Lesser Yellow-headed Vultures) have a very keen sense of smell. They are able to detect a dead carcass from several miles away, long before it starts to rot. Other vultures will often rely on the Turkey Vulture's sense of smell, watching the skies for groups of Turkey Vultures to start circling above a carcass. Once spotted, they will quickly fly to the carcass and chase off the Turkey Vultures. When a large carcass has been found, many types of scavenger will arrive, and a distinct 'pecking' order is observed: eagles and coyotes get the first share, condors next and last in line are the Turkey Vultures and ravens.

With the exception of the Greater and Lesser Yellow-headed Vultures, new world vultures are very gregarious birds. It is not unusual to see groups of up to 200 Black Vultures and Turkey Vultures all feeding together, and groups of over 1000 Black Vultures roosting together.

New world vultures lack a syrinx, the vocal organ used by birds, and so they are voiceless and can only produce faint hissing and grunts by way of sound.

Old World Vultures

There are 15 species of old world vulture found across southern Europe, Africa, the Middle East, and much of Asia. The largest of these is the Monk Vulture, comparable in size to Californian Condors. The smallest is the Hooded Vulture, which is about the size of a raven.

As they are closer relatives of modern diurnal raptors than the new world vultures, the feet of old world vultures are much more suited to grabbing prey. Despite this adaptation, however, with one exception they rarely use their feet to kill their prey, relying mainly on scavenging or feeding on carrion. The exception is the Lappet-faced Vulture, which regularly catches live prey, such as small mammals, and even birds as large as flamingos.

One of the old world vultures – the Palmnut Vulture – is unique amongst birds of prey. While it will eat molluscs, crabs, small mammals, insects, and some carrion, it much prefers a vegetarian diet. Some other

SOCIAL VULTURE

The Black Vulture (*Coragyps atratus*) is the smallest of the new world vultures. Far more social than the slightly larger Turkey Vulture, groups of over 200 have been seen feeding together, with groups of over 1000 sometimes roosting in the same area.

VEGETARIAN CHOICE

A predominantly nut-eating raptor, the Palmnut Vulture (*Gypohierax angolensis*) was once thought to be closely related to the fish eagles. The other common name by which it is known is the Vulturine Fish Eagle, indicating the difficulty ornithologists have had in classifying this bird.

birds of prey do eat small amounts of vegetable matter and grass, but this is the only raptor that relies on fruit, especially the husks of oil palm nuts and raphia fruit, as its staple diet.

Another very large vulture, the Lammergeier, feeds mainly on the bones of carcasses that it finds. Up to 85 percent of its diet can be bones, and if Lammergeiers are unable to crack the bones with their beaks, they will fly high in the sky with the bones and drop them onto the rocks below in order to smash the bones open.

None of the old world vultures has a sense of smell and so they are all dependent on their eyesight to locate their prey. Some vultures, such as Rüppell's Vulture, like to search out thermals and gain height to soar around the skies searching either for their food or to spot other carnivores feeding on a carcass. Others, such as the Egyptian Vulture, prefer low-level flight, quartering out their territory in a style similar to harriers.

Unlike new world vultures, old world vultures all make nests. Usually the nests are quite small to begin with, and they are made from sticks and branches, often lined with grass and dung. When first made, the parent bird frequently dwarfs the nests. The nests tend to be reused in subsequent years, usually being added to and relined. Over a number of years the nests can grow quite large.

Some vultures, such as the White-backed Vulture and the White-rumped Vulture, choose to build their nests in high trees, while others prefer to build their nests on cliff edges. Occasionally, some Himalayan Vultures will take over the nests made in previous years by Lammergeiers, rather than building their own.

As with new world vultures, the clutch size is very small, usually one egg, sometimes two, and very rarely three. Most of the young are fully fledged by about four months after hatching, but some remain dependent on their parents for a further three to four months. The young of the Lammergeier remain dependent on their parents for anywhere up to a year. Many vultures are very gregarious birds, and the young will often stay in the same colonies as the parent birds.

A CREATURE OF HABIT

The Monk Vulture (*Aegypius monachus*), also known as the Cinerous or Black Vulture, is the largest of the old world vultures. Often arriving late at a carcass, they are large enough to dominate and drive off numbers of other smaller vultures that may be feeding.

ENDANGERED GIANT

Opposite: The Andean Condor (*Vultur gryphus*) is the world's largest flying bird with a wingspan in excess of 10ft (3m) and a weight of 24-33lb (11-15kg). Female condors only lay a single egg every other year, and the young take between seven to 11 years to reach sexual maturity. The low rate of reproduction coupled with other factors, such as loss of habitat, disturbance due to tourism, and illegal persecution, are having a severe effect on their numbers.

REBORN IN THE USA

Above: In the 19th century, the Californian Condor (*Gymnogyps californianus*) was found all the way from southwest Canada to northwest Mexico. By the mid-20th century the population had dwindled to around only 60 birds in California. By 1985, at the very point of extinction, it was decided to take all wild birds into captivity and start a breed and release program. Very small colonies of wild birds now exist in areas of California and Arizona and the first wild condor for over 20 years hatched in 2002.

PRETTY UGLY

Opposite: Juvenile King Vultures (*Sarcoramphus papa*) develop their bright garish head colors at around four to five years of age. Like most birds of prey, both males and females are similarly colored.

HEADY PERCH

Above: Living in the tropical forests of South America, the King Vulture spends much of its time perched high in the trees. Very often seen skimming low over the treetops, they are capable of soaring gracefully to great heights. It is thought that King Vultures' brightly-colored heads may help them to identify one another under the dark tree canopies.

FOLLOW YOUR NOSE

Above: The Turkey Vulture (*Cathartes aura*) has the most highly developed sense of smell of any bird of prey. They can detect even well-hidden carrion just by smell. Left: Lacking this heightened sense of smell, Black Vultures (*Coragyps atratus*) watch Turkey Vultures descend to feed and then arrive in large numbers, driving off the Turkey Vultures until they have eaten their fill.

NESTING HABITS

In Europe the main breeding
population of Monk Vultures
(*Aegypius monachus*) is limited to
Spain, where they generally make
large nests in tall trees using sticks.
In the rest of the breeding range
through much of Asia to China, they
may also nest on high mountain
ledges. The nests may be over 6ft
(2m) wide and nearly 10ft (3m) deep
and are often lined with animal skins
and dung.

VULTURE CULTURE

Above: The Hooded Vulture (*Necrosyrtes monachus*) has adapted its feeding habits to the proximity of mankind. Often living very close to human populations, they feed on much of the waste from those communities. Initially sitting and waiting in trees, they will fly down and forage in rubbish dumps as new garbage is added.

SOLITARY SOUTHERNERS

Right: Hooded Vultures are found throughout much of central Africa and parts of southern Africa, and their behavior is different in each region. Below the equator, Hooded Vultures tend to be very solitary, rarely gathering in even small groups. In the more northerly regions they are much more social and gather in groups of hundreds for feeding and roosting.

BONE BREAKER

Left: Also known as the Bearded Vulture, the Lammergeier (*Gypaetus barbatus*) has a rather specialized diet. Waiting patiently at the edge of groups of other feeding vultures, they will then feed on the left-over bones. Smaller bones will be eaten whole, but the larger ones will be broken by dropping them onto rocks from heights of over 150ft (50m). The bones will be repeatedly lifted and dropped until they do break and the fragments are small enough to eat.

DRUGS KILL!

Above: In India between the early 1990s and the first years of the 21st century, the population of White-rumped Vultures (*Gyps bengalensis*) in India plummeted by over 95 percent. The cause was finally traced to drugs used to treat livestock which, when ingested by vultures eating carcasses of the dead animals, caused kidney failure in the birds.

MEAT CLEAVER

Above: The Red-headed Vulture (*Aegypius calvus*) is the only Indian vulture with a beak strong enough to tear open the fresh carcasses of large animals that have recently died. Although other vultures prefer fresh meat to rotting flesh, they usually need to wait for decomposition to start softening the skin before they can tear it open.

BREAKING EGGS

Right: With its long slender beak, the Egyptian Vulture (*Neophron percnopterus*) is more suited to scavenging than to eating carrion. They feed on all manner of garbage, including rotting fruit and even excrement. They will also devour the eggs of large birds, usually breaking them by dropping them onto rocks. Ever resourceful, they have learned that it is easier to break larger eggs by throwing the stones at them.

GREGARIOUS GRIFFONS

Left: Rüppell's Vulture (*Gyps rueppellii*) and above: Griffon Vulture (*Gyps fulvus*). These closely related vultures were previously referred to simply as Griffons – Rüppell's Griffon and the European Griffon. Family members are characterized by their very long necks, highly suited for delving deep into the body of carcasses, and the thick ruffs of feathers at the neckline. They are very gregarious vultures – large groups feed and roost together, often as mixed groups where the territories of different species overlap.

WHEN NIGHT FALLS

Once paired, Hooded Vultures (*Necrosyrtes monachus*) appear to be devoted to each other. Often remaining close to their nesting site, they will commonly roost together in the evenings even outside the breeding season. Their nests are built in trees, carefully lined with fresh greenery during the nesting season, and reused in subsequent years.

A single egg is laid, and the female spends most of her time sitting protectively on it, while being fed by her mate. The young are very weak when they are hatched, and require considerably more parental attention than do most other vulture young.

OWLS

Owls are often referred to as nocturnal raptors to distinguish them from the diurnal raptors, but the description is not entirely accurate. With very few exceptions, diurnal raptors prefer to hunt during daylight, relying mainly on sight to locate their prey. The owl family includes species that span the day in the times that they prefer to hunt, relying on both sight and sound to locate their prey.

Completely unrelated to all diurnal birds of prey, they are another example of 'convergent evolution.' Fossil records date owls back to around 50 million years ago, which makes them contemporaries of the new world vultures. Of all the other species of bird, owls are most closely related to nightjars.

The owl family ranges in size from the very small Elf Owls, Least Pygmy Owls, and Long-whiskered Owlets that are around the size of sparrows and weigh around 1.5oz (43g), up to the magnificent Eurasian Eagle Owl, which is a heavily built, broad-winged bird that weighs up to 9lb (4.1kg) and has a wing span of over 6ft (2m).

With the exception of the Antarctic and the Sahara desert, owls are found throughout the world living and hunting in all types of terrain. The widest ranging of all the owls is the familiar Barn Owl, found throughout North and South America, Europe, most of Africa, India, parts of Asia, and all of Australia.

TWO-WIT TWO-OOO

The Tawny Owl (*Strix aluco*) is very
vocal, and adults use eight to ten
different basic calls. Most famously,
this is the owl that makes the classic
'twit-two-ooo' call. Often this call is
really made by a pair of owls, as the
female starts with a 'ke-wick' call,
which is followed very quickly by the
male's 'hoooo.'

PREVIOUS PAGES

Page 204: Young Snowy Owl (*Bubo
scandiacus*).

Page 205: Long-eared Owl (*Asio otus*).

What really distinguishes owls from the diurnal birds of prey is their
hearing. Below the feathers on their heads, roughly level with their eyes,
their ears are arranged asymmetrically: one ear being slightly higher
than the other. This asymmetry, coupled with side-to-side and twisting
movements of the head, gives them the ability to locate sources of sound
very accurately. While owls have eyesight that is much better than ours
in low levels of light at night, they cannot see in total darkness, but
instead locate and catch their prey by sound alone.

The shape of the face is a very good indicator of how much owls rely
on sound to locate their prey. The beak and the ridge of stiff feathers
surrounding it reflect sound back to the dish-shaped face, which in turn
acts rather like an ear trumpet channeling the sound directly to the ears.
The Great Gray Owl has the most pronounced dish-shaped face of all of
the owls. Spending much of the year living on the edge of the Arctic
tundra, it is quite capable of catching small mammals burrowing under
18in (46cm) of snow, locating them by the sounds that they make as
they move. The owls with perhaps the least well defined facial disk are

those like the Brown Fish Owl which rely on sight to locate their staple prey of fish.

Even during daylight, owls often rely on the sound that their prey makes. When in flight, owls' wings are directly level with their ears. As they often hunt small prey that make hardly any sound, they would lose their ability to locate their prey if their wingbeats were noisy. Consequently, owls have evolved to have completely silent flight. The wing feathers of owls are much softer than those of other birds of prey, and the feathers on the leading edges of the wings have very fine serrations. Both of these adaptations allow some of the air to flow through the feathers, rather than over them, so reducing the noise made by air rushing over the wings. This noiseless flight means that owls can approach their prey in total silence, often catching the victim completely unaware that it is being hunted.

Owls have very large eyes, but lack muscles to move them in the eye sockets. As the eyes are forward-facing, this gives the bird no rearward view. To compensate for this, owls have adapted in two ways. Firstly, they have extra neck vertebrae which allow them both to turn their head much further round and also to be able to twist and tilt it further than other animals. Secondly, the muscles in their necks are very strong, permitting them to twist their heads from one side to the other very quickly. It is the combination of the two adaptations that makes it seem as if an owl can turn its head all the way round from the forward-facing position. In fact, no owl can do this. From the forward-facing position most species of owl can turn their heads at least 180 degrees to look

LOOK INTO MY EYES

As a group, owls hunt throughout the day and night, with individual species specializing at particular times. The eye coloration usually gives a good indication of the preferred time of hunting for the species. Left, above: Yellow-eyed owls, such as the Great Horned Owl (*Bubo virginianus*) prefer to hunt during the daytime. Left, below: Orange-eyed owls like the Indian Eagle Owl (*Bubo bengalensis*) prefer to hunt at dusk and dawn. Above: Dark-eyed owls like this Brown Wood Owl (*Strix leptogrammica*) are generally night-time hunters.

straight behind while the Great Horned Owl is able to turn its head 270 degrees, three-quarters of the way round a full circle. From the furthest extremity in one direction, they are able to turn their heads all the way to the opposite extremity so quickly that it is barely noticeable.

Owls feed on a variety of prey including mammals, insects, reptiles, bats, and birds. Some nocturnal owls will regularly take roosting diurnal raptors. Depending on species, the prey mammals range in size from mice and shrews up to rabbits. Some are even larger than that. A large female Eurasian Eagle Owl is capable of killing a small adult sheep or a roe deer, though this is unusual. Some owls have more specialist diets. Fish owls, as their name suggests, mainly take fish. Others have a more limited diet simply due to the regions they inhabit. For example, the population level of Snowy Owls in the Arctic is known to reflect that of a favored prey, the lemming. In years when lemmings are plentiful, the population of Snowy Owls is high and migration is slow. In years when the lemming population is low, the Snowy Owls migrate very early in search of food.

WHO, ME?

Above: The large head and comparatively small eyes and beak give the Northern Saw-whet Owl (*Aegolius acadicus*) a permanent look of surprise. Its call, sounding very much like a saw being sharpened, gives it its name. At dusk and dawn they hunt for mice, shrews, and voles, and will often catch several in quick succession without eating them, hiding them in safe places to eat later when prey is less abundant.

BIG BIRD

Right: The Eurasian Eagle Owl (*Bubo bubo*) is the largest of all the owl family. Females can weigh anywhere up to 9lb (4.1kg) and have a wingspan of up to 79in (2m). They are active mainly from dusk to dawn. A Eurasian Eagle Owl's flight is noiseless, and soft wingbeats are interspersed with periods of gliding when they are flying over long distances.

Owls nest in a variety of places, such as in holes in trees, on cliff edges, or in hollows in the ground. The Burrowing Owl even nests underground in disused burrows made by prairie dogs and squirrels. They rarely build their own nests, preferring to use nests abandoned by other birds. Owls frequently try to use the same nest sites year after year.

Owls tend to have only a single partner, but they do not always mate for life. The partnership very often only lasts for a single breeding season. The number of eggs that are laid varies between species; anywhere from one to 15 eggs may be laid. In species that lay large numbers of eggs, the number produced in any year is often directly related to the available supply of food. The eggs are laid over a period of days, but incubation starts immediately. This means that the eggs also hatch over a corresponding period of days. The young that hatch first tend have an advantage over their younger siblings, being larger and stronger. They often get the majority of the food and sometimes will even kill the younger nestlings. The surviving chicks usually eat any dead chicks in the nest.

Owls are fully fledged anywhere between four to ten weeks after hatching, the smaller owls often fledging earlier than larger owls. They reach their full adult size at around three to four months of age, and will be fully independent of their parents shortly afterward.

WELL CAMOUFLAGED

The female Snowy Owl (*Bubo scandiacus*) is responsible for incubation of the eggs and early rearing of the young. Nesting on the ground in open areas of the Arctic tundra, in shallow scrapes made by her talons, the strong dark markings on the female help keep her camouflaged while she is on the nest. Nest sites are located near plentiful hunting areas. They must be snow-free, and high enough to command a good view of the surrounding terrain.

BIG PREY, SMALL PREY

Left and above: With their massive and powerful feet, Eurasian Eagle Owls (*Bubo bubo*) can kill animals as large as sheep or roe deer. They usually only do this in times of severe food shortage and generally prey on much smaller mammals, such as rabbits, hares, and even hedgehogs. They will also forage on the ground for small insects and earthworms.

FAIR SHARES

Eurasian Eagle Owls need large open spaces in which to hunt. They have been known to share hunting areas amicably with other raptors, such as Golden Eagles, as the owls hunt from dusk through to dawn, and the eagles hunt during the daytime. Eurasian Eagle Owls have been recorded as living for more than 60 years in captivity. In the wild, their average lifespan is about 20 years. They have no real natural predators and the main causes of death are electrocution from power cables, collision with traffic, and shooting.

WINGED TIGER

Opposite: Great Horned Owls (*Bubo virginianus*) are extremely territorial, both males and females aggressively defending their territory and nesting sites against any potential predators. This is the only species of raptor that is reputed to have killed a human being, possibly while the unfortunate victim was raiding a nest to steal eggs or young.

FROZEN MEALS

Above: Despite its small stature (females measure 6-7.5in/15-19cm in length, with males a little smaller), the Eurasian Pygmy Owl (*Glaucidium passerinum*) can be quite aggressive. With its relatively strong talons, it will often prey on young birds similar in size to itself. It will cache excess prey that it does not need to eat immediately. In winter, it thaws frozen cached prey by warming it under its body.

WORLD'S SMALLEST OWL

Left: The Least Pygmy Owl (*Glaucidium minutissimum*) ranks as the smallest owl in the world, weighing up to 1.8oz (50g) and measuring only 4.5in (11cm) in height. In keeping with its tiny size, it preys on insects and small invertebrates.

HEAR A PIN DROP

The large facial disk of the Great Gray Owl (*Strix nebulosa*) is indicative of the fact that it relies on sound to locate its prey. It is a daytime hunter, and the owl's sensitive hearing enables it to pinpoint the movements of small prey under as much as 18in (46cm) of winter snow.

WINTER COAT

Left: A Great Gray Owl (*Strix nebulosa*). Despite looking bulky, the Great Gray Owl's body is actually relatively small. Much of its apparent size is due to the dense, but light, feathers covering its head and body, which provide excellent insulation against the cold. It preys on small mammals up to the size of rabbits.

TAKE HEART

Above: Barn Owls (*Tyto alba*) are common around the world, being found on all continents with the exception of the Antarctic. Barn Owls and their close relatives, Grass Owls, all have very distinctive heart-shaped faces.

DARKER SHADE OF PALE

Above: With their white breasts and pale golden brown wings, British Barn Owls are the palest in color. Barn Owls from around the rest of the world generally have darker breasts and wings like this European Barn Owl (*Tyto alba guttata*).

LIVE FAST, DIE YOUNG

Right: The average life span of Barn Owls (*Tyto alba*) in the wild is around two years. The young grow to full adulthood rapidly and many breed in their first year at around 10 months old. In years when food is plentiful, as many as 15 eggs may be laid in a single clutch.

PHANTOM OF THE NIGHT

In bright moonlight pale colored Barn Owls stand out very clearly against the dark night sky. With gentle beats of their softly-feathered wings, interspersed with short glides, they fly silently and disappear into the darkness, seeming almost ghost-like.

AGILE CLIMBERS

Left: Young Tawny Owls (*Strix aluco*) sometimes leave the nest before they are fully fledged, often inadvertently falling to the ground. However, the young are remarkably agile and can usually clamber back up to the nest. If they are unable to climb back, the adults continue to feed them while they remain on the ground.

KEEP AN EYE OUT!

Above: During the breeding season, Tawny Owls will often defend their nest sites by attacking intruders. There have been several well-documented cases of people suffering grazed scalps and even losing eyes to aggressive adult owls.

TILL DEATH US DO PART

Above: For its size, the Little Owl (*Athene noctua*) is remarkably long-lived. There are recorded instances of individuals living for more than 15 years in the wild. Little Owls usually mate for life and very often stay together as a pair outside the breeding season.

ECOLOGICALLY SOUND

Right: Little Owls start hunting at dawn and may continue throughout the day until dusk. They prey mainly on insects and occasionally on small mammals. Excess prey is often stored close to the roosting or nesting site. As the flesh rots, it attracts beetles and other small insects to the area, providing a source of further food.

WISE OLD OWL

With relatively large eyes and ears that can occupy over half of their small skulls, owls have fairly small brains. The story of the 'wise old owl' stems from Ancient Greek mythology. A Little Owl (*Athene noctua*) was a constant companion to Athene, the goddess of wisdom, and was considered sacred. Large numbers of Little Owls traditionally nested on the Acropolis in Athens, where the temple of Athene is found.

FAITHFUL FATHER

The male Snowy Owl (*Bubo scandiacus*) is responsible for supplying food to the female during incubation of the eggs, and to the entire family once they are hatched. Often hunting in snowy conditions, the male is far better camouflaged than his mate because he is almost pure white. Snowy Owls mainly prey on lemmings and voles throughout most of their Arctic and wintering range, and newly hatched young are fed boneless and furless pieces of meat. The number of eggs laid by the female is dependent on the availability of food. When food is very scarce, the pair may not mate in that year at all.

WINTER BOOTS

All raptors rely on their feet to catch
their prey. Any injury to their feet will
hamper the bird in its quest for food
and it may eventually starve to death
as a consequence. The Snowy Owl
(*Bubo scandiacus*) has the most
heavily feathered feet of all birds of
prey, as protection against the
extreme Arctic cold.

MOB RULE

Above and right: Hunting both by day and night, the less clearly defined facial disk indicates that this owl relies more on sight than on sound to locate its prey. The presence of a Southern Boobook Owl (*Ninox boobook*) roosting in a tree is often betrayed by constant mobbing by smaller birds using the same site. It is found throughout Australia and is named after its cuckoo-like two syllable call. Recent studies have determined that an almost identical owl found in New Zealand, the Morepork Owl, is actually a separate species in its own right.

234

GONE TO GROUND

Left: The Burrowing Owl (*Athene cunicularia*) is found throughout much of the middle and west of North America and in South America south of the Amazonian forests. Unlike other owls, Burrowing Owls spend most of their time on the ground.

COLONIAL OWL

Below: Unusually for most raptors, Burrowing Owls nest in colonies, with as many as a dozen pairs living in very close proximity. The nests are often built in burrows abandoned by small mammals, although the owls are also able to dig their own burrows. Burrows may extend up to 3ft (1m) below ground, with the entrance surrounded by animal dung. This is thought to deter predators from coming too close as they assume it to be the territorial markings of another predatory animal.

LOW-LEVEL HUNTER

Below: Found across the northern hemisphere and the southern portion of South America, Short-eared Owls (*Asio flammeus*) migrate to the tropics during winter. They prefer to inhabit wide open areas, hunting mainly for small mammals. Prey is normally located by low-level quartering flights over their chosen territory.

TREE HUGGER

Opposite: Long-eared owls (*Asio otus*) are almost completely nocturnal in their hunting habits. During the day, they roost on branches of trees. When approached by a possible predator, a Long-eared Owl will hug close to the tree, stretching its body and wrapping a wing round the trunk to blend in with the bark and camouflage itself. The 'ear' tufts of varying lengths which can be seen on many owls have nothing to do hearing. These long feathers are used partly for camouflage, partly for communication, and also to attract a mate.

ELUSIVE

Left: The Ural Owl (*Strix uralensis*) is widespread, ranging from Scandinavia through central Russia to Japan. It lives mainly in forests well away from inhabited areas and so, despite its wide distribution, it is rarely seen.

SMALL BUT AGGRESSIVE

Above: Although small, and usually preying only on insects, beetles, spiders, and snails, the Pearl-spotted Owlet (*Glaucidium perlatum*) has very large powerful talons for its size. At only 6.5-8in (17-20cm) in length, they are capable of catching and killing birds that are over twice their own size, such as doves.

MILE-HIGH CLUB

Opposite: Western Screech Owls (*Megascops kennicottii*) are found throughout the year from west Canada down the western side of the Rocky Mountains and south into Mexico. Those birds that live and breed at heights of over 8200ft (2500m) above sea-level on the high plateaus of Mexico migrate to lower, warmer regions in winter.

ALONE AGAIN, NATURALLY

Above: Tengmalm's Owl (*Aegolius funereus*), also known as the Boreal Owl, is found across the boreal (coniferously wooded) areas of the northern hemisphere. Nesting usually takes place in holes in trees, often previously made by Black Woodpeckers. Pair-bonding is only for the breeding season, and when the young are fully fledged, the female deserts the male. The following year the male will return to the same nest, but with a different female.

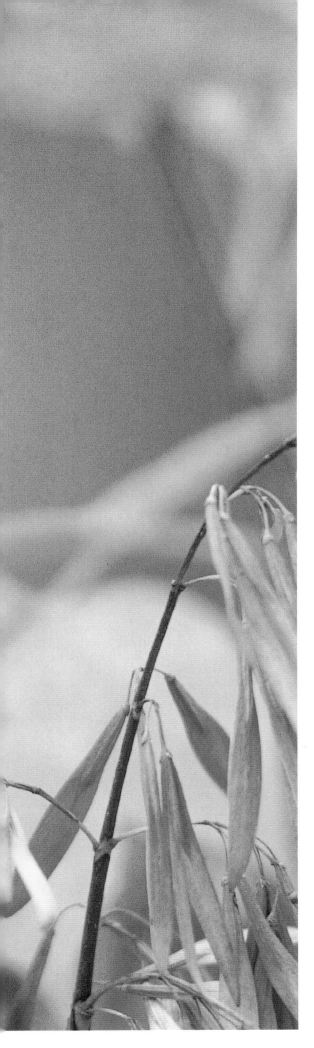

FLAME COLORED

Left: The Flammulated Owl (*Otus flammeolus*) has a rich and complex pattern of feathers which act as excellent camouflage. The flame-colored feathers, from which it gets its name, blend in well with the background when illuminated by the shafts of bright sunlight that penetrate the dense foliage in which it roosts during daylight.

FAMILY TREES

Above: The Striped Owl (*Asio clamator*) was, for a long time, the source of much debate. Until recently, it was considered to be in a unique family, although some ornithologists thought it might be related to the Barn Owl family, while others linked it to the eared owls. Attempts were made to cross-breed Striped Owls with Barn Owls, but the eggs failed to hatch, and it is now accepted to be a close relative of the Long-eared and Short-eared Owls.

IN THE BUFF

Above: When hatched, young Brown
Wood Owls (*Strix leptogrammica*) are
covered in very pale buff-colored
downy feathers. These are gradually
replaced by juvenile feathers which
are similar in marking to the adult
plumage, but lighter.

LEAVE US ALONE

Opposite: Living in dense tropical
woodlands, Brown Wood Owls are
very secretive birds and are rarely
seen. They often roost during the
daytime in pairs, leaning together on
tree branches. When disturbed, they
fly silently deeper into the forests.

SPECTACULAR DUET

Opposite: Spectacled Owls (*Pulsatrix perspicillata*) live mainly in the tropical rain forests of South America. While rarely seen, they are often heard during the breeding season. A pair will call to one another for extended periods of time, performing what sounds like a duet. The male produces a call that resembles a series of pops that gradually become quieter, and this is repeated by the female, but at a higher pitch.

WHAT'S COOKING?

Above: The Barred Owl (*Strix varia*) is fairly common on the eastern side of the United States. The population is growing and spreading through the northwestern regions, where it is now threatening the less common Spotted Owl. The Barred Owl is easily identified by its distinctive call, that sounds very much like 'Who cooks for you, who cooks for you all.'

WHAT?

Above: The nocturnal Indian or Collared Scops Owl (*Otus bakkamoena*) spends the daylight hours hiding in trees, huddling close to tree trunks where it is ideally camouflaged. Although they remain quiet during the daytime, at dusk they start calling. The male birds issue a note that sounds like the word 'What?' every two seconds for anything up to 15 minutes at a time.

A DIFFERENT TUNE

Right: The African Scops Owl (*Otus senegalensis*) was originally thought to be a subspecies of the Common Scops Owl, which is resident in Europe but migrates to Africa during winter. The African Scops Owl is now recognized as a separate species. Ornithologists use their call, a short purring trill, to distinguish between the species.

ATTRACTED TO THE LIGHT

Left: Common Scops Owls (*Otus scops*) are generally woodland-dwelling birds and are often found in trees around villages in rural areas of Europe. They roost during the day, but at night they are often seen hunting near to street lights, as they prey on the insects and moths that are attracted to the light.

DON'T MESS WITH ME

Above: If their roosting is disturbed, Northern White-faced Scops Owls (*Ptilopsis leucotis*) act with aggression, rather than flying off. They jerk their bodies back and forth and make a growling sound. If that fails to scare off the intruder, they bend forward, spread their wings and raise their feathers, making themselves look as big and threatening as possible.

BUFFY THE FISH SLAYER

Left: The Malay Fish Owl (*Bubo ketupa*) is also known as the Buffy Fish Owl, because of its buff coloration. It feeds on a mixed diet of fish, reptiles, amphibians, insects, birds, bats, and carrion. As well as 'still hunting' from a branch, these owls also walk in shallow water snatching at any submerged prey.

IT WAS THIS BIG...

Above: Pel's Fishing Owls (*Scotopelia peli*) hunt from tree branches, watching the surface of nearby water for ripples. The owls glide down from their perches and snatch fish from the surface of the water. As they do not hunt by sound, Fishing Owls lack the adaptations for silent flight that are found in many other owls.

BIG BOYS

Looking far more like hawks than owls, these two species are closely related. Above: The Rufous Owl (*Ninox rufa*) is found in northern Australia and New Guinea. Opposite: The slightly larger Powerful Owl (*Ninox strenua*) is found in southeast Australia. Unlike most other raptors, the males of these two species are much larger than the females. Rufous Owl males weigh between 2.5-3lb (1.1-1.4kg) while females weigh only 1.5-2.5lb (0.7-1.1kg), and Powerful Owl males weigh between 2.5-3.8lb (1.1-1.7kg) while the females tip the scales at 2.2-3.5lb (1-1.6kg).

INDEX